"An immensely valuable resource. . . . There are only a few other introductions to this literature currently available, all of which are either limited in the genres of texts they consider or overly technical. Burke's book does not shy away from introducing students to the complexities of manuscripts and languages of transmission, but he does clearly explain *why* these topics are so essential for fully appreciating the challenges of studying this literature."

— BRENT LANDAU
University of Texas at Austin

"An informative survey of an extensive corpus of Christian apocryphal texts. Burke's prose, written in an engaging and comprehensible style, is particularly accessible to beginning students, but specialists in other aspects of the historical study of religion will also benefit from his succinct description of the field."

— CHARLES W. HEDRICK SR.
Missouri State University

D0897042

Secret Scriptures Revealed

A New Introduction to the Christian Apocrypha

TONY BURKE

WILLIAM B. EERDMANS PUBLISHING COMPANY

GRAND RAPIDS, MICHIGAN / CAMBRIDGE, U. K.

Wm. B. Eerdmans Publishing Co.
2140 Oak Industrial Drive N.E., Grand Rapids, Michigan 49505 /
P.O. Box 163, Cambridge CB3 9PU U.K.

Originally published in Great Britain in 2013 by
Society for Promoting Christian Knowledge, London

19 18 17 16 15 14 13   7 6 5 4 3 2 1

Library of Congress Cataloging-in-Publication Data

Burke, Tony, 1968–
Secret scriptures revealed : a new introduction to the Christian Apocrypha /
Tony Burke.
pages   cm
Includes bibliographical references and index.
ISBN 978-0-8028-7131-2 (pbk. : alk. paper)
1. Apocryphal books (New Testament) — Criticism, interpretation, etc.   I. Title.
BS2840.B87   2013
229'.92061 — dc23
2013031752

Contents

Acknowledgements

Secret Scriptures Revealed is my dream project. My entire professional life has been dedicated to the Christian Apocrypha – beginning with my doctoral work on the *Infancy Gospel of Thomas* and continuing to today with the creation of the York University Christian Apocrypha Symposium Series and the More Christian Apocrypha Project. The texts have informed my teaching also; even in classes that are not part of my courses on New Testament Apocrypha and Gnosticism, I mention apocryphal texts in my lectures as often as possible, though it may seem as though they have little to do with the day's topic. I do this because I think it's important to bring attention to these texts; they form a body of literature that is so important for understanding Christian history and culture. But I also do it because the texts are just plain fun. And I believe strongly that scholars need to share the results of their work with the wider public. So this 'new introduction to the Christian Apocrypha' fulfils many of my goals as a teacher and a scholar. I am truly grateful to SPCK for inviting me to write this book.

My thanks go to my friends, family and colleagues – Laura Cudworth, Ted Cudworth, Brent Landau, Zeba Crook, Lee Martin McDonald, Stephen Shoemaker, and the members of the Kitchener–Waterloo Biblical Colloquium – who read portions of the book and provided feedback. Most of all, I want to thank my editor Lauren Zimmerman for her encouragement, assistance and patience in seeing this project through to its completion.

Secret Scriptures Revealed is dedicated to my teacher Harold Remus, who introduced me to the Christian Apocrypha many years ago and who has been a source of inspiration and support throughout my career.

Tony Burke

1

What are the Christian Apocrypha?

Ten years ago, few people besides biblical studies scholars knew much about apocryphal Christian literature – defined, in short, as stories about Jesus and his contemporaries similar to New Testament texts but, for one reason or another, not included in the Bible. I remember awkward situations at parties when non-academics would ask me what I did for a living. Nothing could kill a conversation faster than saying, 'I study apocryphal gospels.'

But that all changed in 2004 with the publication of Dan Brown's novel *The Da Vinci Code*. For the few people in the world who have not read the book or seen the 2006 blockbuster film adaptation, *The Da Vinci Code* is the rarest kind of best-seller: a religious thriller. The plot hinges on the murder of a member of a group charged to safeguard the secret of the Holy Grail – here explained, not literally as the chalice used by Jesus at the last supper, but symbolically as Mary Magdalene, the woman who carried the bloodline of Jesus. That's right: the novel says she was Jesus' wife and mother of his only child. The details of this shocker are revealed in the novel through readings from apocryphal gospels. In the *Gospel of Philip*, Mary Magdalene is named as the 'spouse' of Jesus, and we read that he 'used to kiss her often on her mouth'. And according to the *Gospel of Mary Magdalene*, Jesus charged Mary, not the 'sexist' apostle Peter, to carry on his Church. We learn also about the existence of 'more than eighty gospels', many of which describe the ministry of Jesus 'in very human terms'. These gospels were censored by the Church, which sought, for political reasons, to portray Jesus, not as a man, but as the Son of God.

These statements, though certainly shocking, are not entirely new. *The Da Vinci Code* is one of over 40 'secret scrolls' novels that use apocryphal texts, whether real or imagined, as the crux of their plots. What, then, made Brown's novel so different, and so successful? The answer comes in the opening page of the book, which lists several points as 'fact', and asserts that 'all descriptions of artwork, architecture, documents, and secret rituals in this novel are accurate'. Could this be true? Do apocryphal gospels, suppressed by the Church for centuries, really say that Jesus was just a man, that he was married, had a child, and that the Church founded in his name was stolen from his rightful successor? Readers of *The Da Vinci Code* were desperate for answers. Books were written both supporting and challenging Brown's claims. Churches scrambled to prevent wide-scale abandonment of the faith by forming study groups to channel interest in the book into re-engagement with the Church. And Christian Apocrypha scholars found themselves thrust into the spotlight by news media eager for a response to the furore.

The excitement over the Christian Apocrypha continued to build with the publication of the long-lost *Gospel of Judas* in 2006. The team of scholars who worked on the text claimed that it portrayed Judas as a hero, not a villain, and the team used the discovery to add fuel to the fire of one of Brown's arguments that 'history is always a one-sided account . . . written by the winners'. The *Gospel of Judas* represented one of many forms of early Christianity, each with its own, equally valid views on Jesus, but not the views of the 'winners' who compiled the New Testament. Then, in 2012, news media and internet bloggers debated the authenticity of the *Gospel of Jesus' Wife*, a newly revealed fragment from an ancient text in which Jesus is asked by his disciples about Mary (likely Mary Magdalene), whom Jesus appears to refer to as his 'wife'. For better or worse, the Christian Apocrypha have become an indelible part of popular consciousness. Not only that; they're downright sexy.

As it turns out, many of Dan Brown's claims about the Christian Apocrypha are not 'fact' at all. The texts he uses to advance the plot do not portray Mary Magdalene as the wife of Jesus. Nor do they portray Jesus as entirely human. In fact, the gospels of Philip and Mary establish that Jesus is more divine than his biblical counterpart, not less, and are related to a form of Christianity that encouraged sexual abstinence. Brown's historical faux pas (and there are many) have been a source of much irritation for biblical scholars and historians, but they are more distracting than destructive – *The Da Vinci Code* is only a novel, after all. What is truly disturbing is the reaction to the book from non-specialists in the field. Most of the books and articles critical of the Christian Apocrypha are written by North American evangelicals eager to champion the New Testament as containing the truth about the life and teachings of Jesus and as representing the accurate history of the early Church. They call for their readers to keep away from apocryphal texts; one writer even declares that scholars of the Christian Apocrypha, 'though bright and sincere, are not merely wrong; they are misled. They are oblivious to the fact that they are being led down this path by the powers of darkness.' Not content with merely pointing out problems with Brown's version of the history of the Church, or with the sensational claims some-times made by legitimate Christian Apocrypha scholars, modern critics of the Christian Apocrypha want to smother conversation on the texts by pushing them back into the margins of history. They characterize the Apocrypha as late texts, not early; written to destroy Christianity – to promote error, not truth. They are fakes, forgeries and fictions.

It is an old strategy. Writers of the Church have made the same arguments for centuries. One of the earliest is Athanasius, the fourth-century Bishop of Alexandria in Egypt. In 367 CE he wrote to the churches of his domain, warning them that they should accept only the 27 books of the New Testament as Scripture and that

> There should be no mention at all of apocryphal books created by heretics, who write them whenever they want but try to bestow favor on them by assigning them dates, that by setting them forth as ancient, they can be, on false grounds, used to deceive the simple minded. *(Festal Letter* 39.7)

Not everyone agreed with Athanasius, because apocryphal texts continued to be copied, read and written over the centuries. Stories from the Christian Apocrypha appear in sermons, art, iconography, drama, poetry and song, contributing to Christian tradition despite considerable efforts to eradicate the texts.

But few people today consider any apocryphal texts to be sacred, authoritative writings. Outside of scholarship, most people encounter them in works by writers, artists or filmmakers and, for the most part, these works use the texts to construct conspiracy theories such as we find in *The Da Vinci Code*. These conspiracy theories appeal to the mistrust many feel towards traditional institutions – religious, social or political – and they have led the curious to seek out apocryphal texts and read them for themselves. This spirit of inquiry has been met with arguments that the Apocrypha are corrosive to the reader's faith and endanger the soul. Despite such attempts to censure the literature, today also there is plenty of 'mention . . . of apocryphal books', and I hope you will agree, we are richer for it.

The book you hold in your hands, *Secret Scriptures Revealed*, was written as a response to all of this conflict over the significance of the Christian Apocrypha. It is intended for those who have become interested in apocryphal texts and now seek a guide through the literature. In many bookstores, and certainly most libraries, a visitor can find collections and studies of apocryphal Christian texts. No longer suppressed, the Christian Apocrypha are available now to anyone who seeks them. But the scholarly collections and critical editions can be intimidating and inaccessible to newcomers – indeed, much of the in-depth scholarship is difficult to find even in major university libraries, and little of it is composed in English. And works targeted for a more general readership tend to suffer from a lack of impartiality, with both 'liberal' scholars and 'conservative' theologians couching their arguments in hyperbole – the texts portray Jesus as more human; no, he is more divine; the texts are earlier than those in the New Testament; no, they are all much later; etc. – leaving readers wondering how the writers can be so divided. The reality, of course, is far more nuanced. The texts are not all early or all late, their portrayals of Jesus not all more human or all more divine. Each text has its own story and its own contribution to make to our understanding of Christian history.

This book aims to cut through the rhetoric of the texts' champions and opponents and present a sober discussion of the material that will, hopefully, encourage an appreciation for the literature. But not belief. Ideally, scholars try, as much as possible, to study history with detachment, setting aside judgements and biases about the subjects of their study and supporting their arguments with evidence from appropriate sources. The Christian Apocrypha need to be studied with that same level of objectivity, not to prove they are superior or inferior to other types of Christian literature, not to call for the replacement of canonical texts with non-canonical, or for avoidance or censorship of unofficial scripture. The goal of this study, then, is to inform readers, not to convince. If there is a message for readers to take from this book it is only that all views, no matter how challenging, deserve to be heard, that no writing should be prohibited, that nothing is more dangerous to freedom than the suppression of ideas.

This opening chapter of *Secret Scriptures Revealed* provides readers with the background necessary for understanding apocryphal literature. Key terms are defined, such as 'apocrypha', 'canon', 'orthodoxy', 'heresy' and 'Gnosticism' – all somewhat slippery but nevertheless important for what follows. The second chapter will acquaint readers with aspects of the scholarly study of the Christian Apocrypha, in particular how texts are recovered and reconstructed so that they can be made available to other scholars and readers. The chapter also traces the dispersion of the texts over the centuries, in various languages and sources, up to their inclusion in Christian Apocrypha collections in use today. After these preliminary matters, we will look at the apocryphal texts themselves, working chronologically through the early decades of Christianity. Chapter 3 begins with the birth of Jesus and continues through his career as a teacher and miracle-worker; Chapter 4 focuses on his death and post-resurrection appearances to his disciples; and Chapter 5 looks at the missionary journeys of the apostles, and other legends of eminent Christian figures. In these three chapters we cover a large number of texts, more than in any other introduction to the Christian Apocrypha. The other introductions have a much more narrow mandate – either focusing exclusively on gospels, or restricting themselves to early texts – whereas this book casts its net wide to offer readers a look at some rarely studied writings. For those looking to explore the material further, each chapter includes acknowledgements of sources, and suggestions for additional reading. The final section of the book returns to the discussion of the reception of the Christian Apocrypha today with a series of questions addressing misconceptions about the texts born out of their treatment in popular media (such as *The Da Vinci Code*), and subsequent reactions to these treatments.

It is hoped that readers will finish the book with an awareness of the wide range of apocryphal Christian texts and what they have to contribute to our knowledge of Christian thought and history. Far too often these texts are dismissed as forgeries and fictions, but they need to be taken seriously as vital witnesses to beliefs and practices from throughout Christian history and as products of human imagination that continue to enthral readers.

Sources and studies (complete bibliographical information for each entry can be found in the bibliography at the end of the book)

Quotations from *The Da Vinci Code* are taken directly from Brown's novel. For an overview of other 'secret scrolls' novels, see Robert M. Price, *Secret Scrolls*. The statement that Christian Apocrypha scholars are 'misled' by 'the powers of darkness' is made by Ben Witherington in *The Gospel Code*, p. 174. This and other conservative reactions to current interest in the Christian Apocrypha are surveyed in my article 'Heresy Hunting in the New Millennium'.

What does 'apocrypha' mean?

The term *apocrypha*, or the singular *apocryphos/apocryphon*, is a Greek word meaning 'secret', 'hidden' or 'mysterious'. The term 'Christian Apocrypha' designates non-biblical Christian literature that features tales of Jesus, his family and his immediate followers. They are similar in content and genre to texts included in the New Testament; the essential difference is that they were not selected for inclusion in the Bible, either because those who decided on the Bible's contents did not approve of them, or because they were composed after the time of this selection process.

Use of the word *apocrypha* in antiquity was somewhat fluid. It could be used positively by some, including practitioners of magic but also Christians and Jews, for their own 'secret books'. Two Christian books use the term explicitly in their titles: the *Apocryphon* (or *Secret Book*) *of John* and the *Apocryphon of James*. However, critics of such texts used the term pejoratively. Irenaeus, the Bishop of Lyons (writing around 180 CE), for example, used *apocryphos* to designate a writing that he considered forged or false. Other writers used it interchangeably with the term *antilegomena*: texts that were not considered Scripture, but were nevertheless edifying and could be read in private or in study. In modern speech we may call a story or event 'apocryphal' if we are unsure that it is true.

To complicate matters, the term *apocrypha* is applied also to a group of writings sandwiched between the Old Testament and the New Testament in some Bibles. These texts derive from the Septuagint, an early Greek translation of the Hebrew Scriptures made between the third and first centuries BCE. The Septuagint includes a number of texts – such as 1 Maccabees, Sirach and a longer version of Daniel – not accepted into the Hebrew Bible when its contents were firmly established in the second century CE. But early Christian writers principally wrote in Greek, not Hebrew; so when they wished to draw upon stories from Jewish Scripture, they used the Septuagint or other Greek translations. By the fifth century, however, churches in the West preferred to read their sacred texts in Latin. Pope Damasus commissioned Jerome (347–420) to create a single, official Latin translation of the Bible, known later as the 'Vulgate' (or 'popular' version). For the Old Testament material, Jerome wanted to translate the texts directly from Hebrew, rather than Greek. When he discovered that some of the texts in the Greek Septuagint had no Hebrew counterpart, Jerome suggested that these texts should be set apart from the other writings, since Jews outside of Egypt apparently did not consider them sacred.

Not everyone agreed with Jerome; so it wasn't until the early sixteenth century that a Bible was printed that was arranged according to Jerome's suggestion. It was at this time that the books set apart from the Old and New Testaments acquired the name 'Apocrypha'. The influential King James Version followed suit, but most modern Protestant Bibles omit the texts entirely. Roman Catholic and Greek Orthodox churches disregard Jerome and continue to include all the texts of the Septuagint in their Old Testament, though under the designation 'Deutero-canonical' (meaning 'belonging to the second canon').

There are yet other Jewish books that are not part of the Old Testament, such as the books of *Enoch*, *Jubilees*, and various testaments of the patriarchs (e.g. the *Testament of Abraham*). These are texts that were read by Jews and Christians in antiquity but rarely achieved authoritative status – the inclusion of *1 Enoch* and *Jubilees* in the Ethiopic Bible is a notable exception. Scholars distinguish these writings from the Apocrypha of the Old Testament by placing them in the category of Pseudepigrapha (or writings 'with false superscription'), a problematic term given that many texts within the Bible are also pseudepigraphical – that is, they were each written by someone other than the person whose name is upon it.

Unlike the Apocrypha of the Old Testament, which have a semi-scriptural status, the texts of the Christian Apocrypha are rarely considered edifying by any Christian group today. And though the texts are often referred to as the 'New Testament Apocrypha', they do not constitute a standard collection of literature like the Apocrypha of the Old Testament. The closest analogy to the Old Testament Apocrypha in Christian-authored literature is the body of texts published today as 'the Apostolic Fathers'. These are texts written in the late first and early second centuries by post-apostolic Church writers (that is, they are not attributed to apostles, as we often find in apocryphal texts). They include the *Didache*, *Barnabas*, the letters of Ignatius, the *Shepherd of Hermas*, *1* and *2 Clement*, and others. Some of these texts were considered for inclusion in the Bible, and some even appear alongside the standard 27 books of the New Testament in a few important early Bible manuscripts.

Sources and studies

For a recent, authoritative collection of the Apostolic Fathers, see the edition of Michael E. Holmes. The Pseudepigrapha are available in the two volumes edited by James H. Charlesworth and a supplementary collection edited by Richard Bauckham, James Davila and Alexander Panayotov. Though this material features Old Testament/ Hebrew Bible figures, some of the texts contain additions made by Christian copyists, while others were written entirely by Christians (e.g. the *Martyrdom and Ascension of Isaiah*, the *Odes of Solomon*, perhaps *Joseph and Aseneth*) and thus, in a sense, can also be considered Christian Apocrypha.

What makes these texts 'apocryphal'?

A text is apocryphal because it was not chosen to be part of the canon. The term 'canon' means 'norm' or 'standard' or, more concretely, 'measuring stick'. In the religious context, it refers to standard, authoritative doctrine or teaching, but it became applied also to the Bible as an expression of that authoritative doctrine and, more narrowly, to the list of books contained in the Bible. Other disciplines use the term in the same way for lists of works that they value – 'the western canon', for example, refers to the art, music and literature important in western culture (such as Picasso, Beethoven and Shakespeare); the 'film canon' refers to the motion picture masterpieces against which all other films are judged (including *Citizen Kane* and *Doctor Strangelove*). Because the adjective 'apocryphal' is often used negatively, scholars sometimes prefer to use the less value-laden term 'non-canonical' alongside 'canonical' to describe the full range of early Christian literature.

The New Testament canon in most areas of the Christian world is comprised of 27 separate texts. The earliest of these texts are not gospels, as one might assume, but letters. In fact, the majority of the New Testament – 22 out of the 27 texts – consists of letters. Thirteen are attributed to the apostle Paul. Between 35 and 62 CE (or thereabouts), Paul travelled to cities in Asia Minor (modern Turkey), Greece and Italy, preaching his 'gospel' and establishing churches. Most of Paul's letters were written in response to problems encountered by these churches in his absence. Unfortunately, the letters reveal little about the substance of Paul's preaching about Jesus. When he uses the term 'gospel' (from the Greek *euangelion*, meaning 'good news'), Paul refers not to a written text about Jesus' life and teachings but to his views on membership in the Christian community (Paul seems to have been the first apostle to preach to non-Jews) and practice (to circumcise or not to circumcise, that is the question).

Scholars are divided about which of Paul's letters were truly written by the apostle, and which were written in his name. All agree that Paul wrote Galatians, 1 Thessalonians, 1 and 2 Corinthians, Philippians, Philemon and Romans (the seven 'undisputed' letters), and most consider 1 and 2 Timothy and Titus (the

'Pastoral Epistles') to be pseudepigraphical, but the authorship of 2 Thessalonians, Colossians and Ephesians is still disputed. The other New Testament letters – 1 and 2 Peter, James, Jude, the three letters of John, and Hebrews – are widely considered to be relatively late texts, composed perhaps as late as 100–125 CE; therefore, they could not be written by apostles of Jesus and must be either pseudonymous (written in someone else's name; e.g. 1 and 2 Peter, Jude), homonymous (written by someone with the same name as an early Christian leader; e.g. James) or anonymous (John's letters are actually attributed to 'the elder' – see for example 2 John 1 – and Hebrews does not identify its author at all).

The New Testament Gospels bear the names of apostles (Matthew and John) or disciples of apostles (Mark and Luke) but the majority of scholars believe they were originally anonymous. It is likely that Mark was composed first – between 66 and 70 CE, the time of the Roman siege of Jerusalem that ended with the destruction of the Temple. Mark constructed his Gospel using orally circulating tales and teachings of Jesus and perhaps a few written accounts. With Mark we get the earliest association of the word 'gospel' (or 'good news', see Mark 1.1) with a biography of Jesus, though Mark's life of Jesus has some major gaps – it begins, not with Jesus' birth, but with his baptism as an adult, and promises that Jesus has risen from death but provides no resurrection appearance stories.

Perhaps Matthew and Luke, written around 80–90 CE, were created to redress Mark's deficiencies. Each includes its own birth story (or 'infancy narrative') and resurrection appearances, as well as other tales not found in Mark. A large chunk of this new material, principally teachings, is shared by Matthew and Luke, leading scholars to speculate that they both incorporate in their texts a now-lost written collection of sayings of Jesus. This collection has been dubbed 'the Sayings Source' or simply 'Q' (an abbreviation of the German word *Quelle*, meaning 'source'). Given that Mark, Matthew and Luke have much material in common, scholars have come to call them the Synoptic Gospels, because together (*syn*) they see (*optic*) the life of Jesus very much the same way.

Rounding out the New Testament Gospels is the Gospel of John, dated usually to around 100 CE. John differs considerably from the Synoptic Gospels. Here Jesus is portrayed as the pre-existent Word (Greek: *logos*) of God who takes on human form. He tells no parables, heals no lepers and says very little about the kingdom of God. Instead he speaks at great length about himself: he is the good shepherd, the bread of life, the light of the world.

Also included in the New Testament is the Acts of the Apostles, written by the same author as the Gospel of Luke and detailing the activities of the apostles after Jesus' death up to Paul's journey to Rome around 60 CE. And last is Revelation, also known as the Apocalypse of John, in which a Christian visionary witnesses a cosmic battle between good and evil that will occur when Jesus returns to bring God's kingdom to earth.

How and when did the western Church select the texts for the New Testament? Contrary to popular belief, the Bible did not drop down fully formed from the heavens at the end of the first century. It took a considerable amount of time for Christians to decide which books were to be considered Scripture. We have no official records detailing the selection process, but early Church writings provide hints at why some texts were included and some were not.

First, there is a concern about authority. The text must be attributed to an apostle of Jesus or a companion of an apostle in order to be considered trustworthy. But apocryphal texts are also attributed to apostles and other early Christian figures, and both ancient writers and modern scholars question the authorship of some New Testament texts; so apostolic authority cannot be the only criterion.

The church historian Eusebius of Caesarea (263–339 CE) gives us more insight into how the books were chosen. He writes of the rejected books,

> No one standing in the succession of the true churches ever thought it worthwhile to mention any of these in any of his treatises. And their literary character differs greatly from the style characteristically found in the apostolic writings; while the opinions they express and their choice of material clearly reveal that they are as different as possible from truly orthodox works, since they are, after all, fabrications of heretics.
>
> (*Ecclesiastical History* 3.25.7)

11

The official Christian Scriptures, then, must have antiquity – that is, they must have been held in esteem by early Church writers. Of course, Eusebius means church writers with whom he and his peers agree.

This brings us to Eusebius's other criterion: the contents of accepted texts must reflect the beliefs of the community. And they do so because the community was formed and has grown through the use of those texts as missionary guides and resources for debate. Their identity is interwoven with those texts. Disputes arose, however, when one Christian community encountered another that valued other writings, and a decision had to be made about whether or not to adopt the new texts as their own. The New Testament is the end product, then, of various Christian communities joining together, reaching consensus on their beliefs and combining the books that reflect those beliefs. Why else would the New Testament contain not one but four Gospels?

Reaching a consensus was a complicated process. At first only the Hebrew Scriptures (in Greek form) were valued by Christians. They searched these texts for passages they could use to show that Jesus was the promised Messiah. Such passages may have been compiled in what are called Testimonia collections, so that they could be readily at hand when preaching or writing. But before long, Christian-penned texts took on a special status. This happened first for the letters of Paul, which seem to have been assembled in a standard collection by the late first century.

The process took longer with the Gospels. Up until the middle of the second century, stories and sayings of Jesus that circulated by word of mouth seem to have been valued over written texts. Even when a gospel, or 'the gospel', is mentioned by early Church writers it is unclear if a written text is intended or what text that might be, since many gospels, even those that became canonical, started out as anonymous texts. To complicate matters further, early quotations by Church writers from 'the gospel' often don't match our modern texts, but instead appear to have been drawn from 'harmonies' – texts combining readings from multiple gospels. Harmonies may have been born out of criticism from non-Christians over the existence of multiple, competing versions of Jesus' life and teachings. The most famous harmony from this time period is that of Tatian, a Syrian who came to Rome to study with the famed Christian apologist Justin Martyr in the mid-second century. Tatian created the *Diatessaron*, meaning 'through the four', a combination of Matthew, Mark, Luke and John, and perhaps other sources. He took his harmony back with him to Syria where, as the 'Gospel of the Mixed', it was authoritative until its replacement in the fifth century by the four separate Gospels.

Another solution to the problem of multiple gospels was offered around the same time by Marcion of Sinope, who adopted only one gospel as scripture. In fact, Marcion is credited with establishing the first Christian-only collection of scripture (that is, without the Hebrew texts of the Old Testament). This collection featured only the Gospel of Luke and ten of the letters of Paul (excluding 1 and 2 Timothy, and Titus). But these were apparently edited to reflect Marcion's distinct theology, which entailed a rejection of Jewish texts and traditions. Thus Luke's recounting of Jesus' birth, which is heavily indebted to stories from Hebrew Scripture, is eliminated from Marcion's gospel. Like Tatian's *Diatessaron*, Marcion's collection of texts was highly popular in some Christian centres.

It is perhaps in reaction to Tatian and Marcion that the early Church Father Irenaeus of Lyons presented his justification for adopting the four canonical Gospels as authoritative. He writes,

> The Gospels could not possibly be either more or less in number than they are. Since there are four zones of the world in which we live, and four principal winds, while the Church is spread over all the earth, and the pillar and foundation of the Church is the gospel, and the Spirit of life, it fittingly has four pillars, everywhere breathing out incorruption and revivifying men. From this it is clear that the Word, the artificer of all things, being manifested to men gave us the gospel, fourfold in form but held together by one Spirit. (*Against Heresies* 3.11.8)

So Irenaeus is effectively asserting the authority of multiple Gospels over one (Marcion's), and separate Gospels over a harmony (Tatian's). Irenaeus is also the first known writer who clearly and explicitly appeals to the four New Testament Gospels by name.

13

But what of the other texts that ended up in the New Testament? Irenaeus's works indicate that he valued the four Gospels, most of the letters of Paul, Acts, 1 and 2 John, and 1 Peter, along with the *Shepherd of Hermas* and, today included in the Old Testament Apocrypha, the Wisdom of Solomon. He identifies as 'disputed' Philemon, Hebrews, James, Jude, 2 Peter, 3 John, Revelation and the *Apocalypse of Peter*. A more formal canon list, known as the Muratorian Canon, composed perhaps in Rome in the late second century, is quite similar, though it stipulates that *Hermas*, Wisdom and the *Apocalypse of Peter* can be read only in private. What this tells us is that, at the close of the second century, the canon was still in flux. Irenaeus and the Muratorian Canon reflect the esteem held by some western Christian thinkers for many of the texts found today in the New Testament; but the status of some, particularly the Catholic letters (a term for the non-Pauline letters) and Revelation, is in dispute, while others eventually excluded from the collection are acknowledged as Scripture. In other communities, the early canon is far less well documented; indeed, some Christian groups may have resisted the very idea of limiting the texts available to be read.

Additional canon lists and discussions of the canon appear in the third, fourth and fifth centuries. As late as Eusebius of Caesarea, writing around 311, some of the Catholic letters and Revelation remain in dispute, but *Hermas* and *Peter* are declared spurious, and other texts, such as the *Gospel of Peter* and the *Acts of Andrew*, are unequivocally eliminated as 'absurd and godless' (*Ecclesiastical History* 3.3.5–7; 3.25.1–7). The 27-book collection widely known today is described for the first time in 367 in the *Thirty-ninth Festal Letter* of Athanasius, the Bishop of Alexandria, though even Athanasius allowed the *Didache* and *Hermas* still to be read in private. The quasi-canonical status of these and other texts of the Apostolic Fathers is reflected also in two important biblical manuscripts of the time: the Codex Sinaiticus of the fourth century includes *Barnabas* and *Hermas*, and the Codex Alexandrinus of the fifth century adds *1* and *2 Clement*.

Of course, Athanasius's decree, supported by the powerful Bishop of Rome, only had authority in the domain of the western Roman Empire. In the eastern part of the empire, the Greek churches did not come to firm agreement on including Revelation in the Bible until the tenth century. And other variations occurred in Syria, Armenia and Egypt. The most dramatic differences are found in the Ethiopic Church. Even today, its Bible includes several texts relating to church organization and practice, along with the *Book of the Covenant* (containing a post-resurrection discourse by Jesus to his disciples), the *Book of the Rolls,* and others. All of these variations mean that we need to be careful when discussing the canon of the New Testament, and in referring to books as 'canonical' and 'non-canonical'. Canonical status varies over time and place. The situation gets murkier still with several more recent developments, including Martin Luther's attempt to remove several of the Catholic letters and Revelation from the Bible (Hebrews, James, Jude and Revelation are still placed last in German Lutheran Bibles today) and the expanded canon of the Church of Latter-Day Saints. All of that said, for the sake of ease, I will use the term 'canonical' from here on as a term for texts of the 27-book collection that is most familiar to English readers.

We need to be careful also of making too much of the distinction between canonical and non-canonical Christian texts. Despite the Church's efforts to suppress apocryphal texts, many of them never really went away. They continued to be created, copied, read, used as inspiration for art and literature, and published up to today. They have continued to survive for one very practical reason: the New Testament simply does not provide enough information about the lives of Jesus, his family and his followers to satisfy believers' curiosity, nor does it answer every question believers may have about life here on earth and life in the hereafter. Writers of apocryphal texts also recognized the value of using narrative – story – to formulate their ideas and communicate those ideas to a wide audience. Official texts and unofficial legends worked hand in hand over the centuries to mould and shape Christian thought and practice. Biblical and non-biblical imagery and stories meet in iconography. Apocryphal legends of the apostles are read on feast days for the saints. And teachings bearing upon the conception of Jesus are reflected in texts about the birth and upbringing of his mother Mary.

For the vast majority of believers, who could neither read nor understand much of what they heard read from Latin scriptures, the distinction between the New Testament and 'apocryphal books' held little meaning. Arguably, the line was drawn only with the creation of the first printed Bible in 1456. With this innovation, Bibles in the vernacular became increasingly more available and literacy increased. Now what constituted official Scripture was clear, and apocryphal texts became less an expression of current popular piety and more an object of interest for scholars of ancient and medieval Christianity. So the texts, most of them anyway, were never 'lost', though their value, their function and their audiences certainly have changed over time. Nevertheless, Christianity has had, and continues to have, its loud voices calling for the avoidance or destruction of texts that do not meet its approval.

Sources and studies

The Muratorian Canon and other canon lists discussed here are included in Bart Ehrman, *Lost Scriptures*, pp. 330–42. For more on the canon selection process, by an eminent scholar in the field, see Lee Martin McDonald's books, *The Formation of the Bible* and *The Origin of the Bible*.

Reconstructing 'heretical' Christianity

As Dan Brown argues in *The Da Vinci Code*, history is written by the winners. Their perspective alone colours the accounts of all the great battles, momentous events and heated debates. The same can be said for the history of early Christianity and its impact on the reception of apocryphal texts. The 'winners' of early Christian history, at least from the western perspective, are the churches under the authority of Rome and Constantinople in the fourth century. They determined the shape of the canon; they determined what was the correct teaching; they even determined who was an acceptable teacher. The 'losers' were those Christian communities or individuals who valued different texts and different teachings, and followed different teachers. Battles are won by the group with the most power, not necessarily the group that is most virtuous or correct. And when it comes to early Christian history, there are compelling reasons to question the authority of the winners and their claim, indeed anyone's claim, to represent the 'true' teachings of Jesus.

Rome and Constantinople, with their eminent champions Irenaeus, Eusebius, Athanasius, and others, called themselves the 'orthodox', a term which means literally '[having] right belief'. Anyone who did not agree with the orthodox was declared a heretic, from a Greek word meaning 'choice' (because heretics are those who have 'chosen' to deviate from the 'truth'). Of course, orthodoxy is in the eye of the beholder – everyone thinks that he or she is the one who has it right. No one calls oneself a heretic; indeed, we even have one apocryphal text, the Coptic *Revelation of Peter*, in which the writer declares himself orthodox and his opponents are called heretics. In another early Christian text, the *Testimony of Truth*, one heretical (that is, non-orthodox) writer asserts his orthodoxy (his 'true testimony') over other heretics. Even today, the title 'orthodox' is used within Christianity and Judaism when a group wishes to distinguish itself as correct, or more traditional in its practices and beliefs than other groups.

The orthodox of antiquity justified their position of dominance by tracing an unbroken line of succession from Jesus through the apostles, their disciples, and so on up to the leaders of the Church in the fourth century. The 'right belief' thus had been preserved inviolate. The heresies, they said, originated from the introduction of outside influences, such as Platonism, Judaism, and other systems, via false teachers intent on corrupting the faith. To the orthodox, the Christian story is a progression from unbelief (pre-Christian Judaism and Graeco-Roman 'paganism') to right belief (the arrival of Christianity) to wrong belief (heresies). And the orthodox seek to return Christianity to right belief.

This official account of the Church's history has been challenged vigorously by scholars over the past century, but none have done so more effectively and provocatively than Walter Bauer. In 1934, Bauer wrote *Rechtgläubigkeit und Ketzerei im ältesten Christentum*, translated into English (after much delay) in 1971 as *Orthodoxy and Heresy in Earliest Christianity*. Bauer's claim was that, in some areas of the ancient world, orthodox Christianity arrived late. The earliest form of Christianity in these areas was one of the so-called heresies and, in some cases, this form remained dominant for centuries before the infiltration of orthodoxy. When orthodoxy did arrive, it would have been considered a heresy, and what was later called 'heresy' was originally orthodox. We get some hint of this phenomenon already in the New Testament. The book of Acts portrays the spread of the Christian message as emanating out from Jerusalem carried by the original apostles of Jesus. But Acts says nothing about the origins of Christianity in Rome – a Christian community is already established before Paul arrives there in Acts 28.14 – and nothing is said at all about communities in Syria and Egypt, two very important centres of Christianity by the late second century. Presumably this is because the author of Acts, who is certainly 'orthodox' by modern standards, had no ties to these communities. Bauer's study takes Acts as a starting point and then brings in various other early Church writings to trace the growth of Christianity in all the major regions in which it took hold, including Greece, Italy and Asia Minor.

The Bauer Thesis, as it is called, has been attacked by critics for failing to prove itself for many of these regions. And, to be fair, new evidence for heretical Christian groups not available to Bauer when he wrote his book has eroded his arguments. Nevertheless, Bauer's work on Syrian Edessa remains persuasive, and his larger point, that orthodox Christianity's story of its origins should not go unchallenged, cannot be ignored. The influence of Bauer is seen in the work of a number of scholars in the USA, including Helmut Koester, Elaine Pagels and Bart Ehrman. They continue to champion the notion that Christianity, from the very start, was multiform and only later did it achieve uniformity. Ehrman, in particular, emphasizes development in early Christianity with his use of the term 'proto-orthodox' to describe the views of writers of the second and third centuries that were declared 'orthodox' in the fourth and later centuries. His point is that even the orthodoxy of the fourth-century Church did not entirely exist earlier, but developed over time, sometimes working out its beliefs and practices (including the formation of the New Testament) in opposition to innovations made by 'heretics'.

The ramifications of the Bauer Thesis are that no group from early Christianity has the exclusive right to declare itself the 'true' form of the faith. All of the communities claim to have the right teaching, all of them can trace their beliefs back through certain apostles to Jesus himself, all of them value texts attributed to or featuring stories of esteemed early Christian figures, and all of them claim the other Christian groups have it all wrong. This determination does not mean we admit paralysis and abandon the effort to reconstruct early Christian history, but it is an acknowledgement that there is much we do not know about the beginnings of Christianity and that we cannot accept one group's version of history and set of beliefs as correct simply because they triumphed over the others. All Christian groups have something to tell us about early Christian history and, by extension, every piece of Christian literature is worthy of study, whether it was written by the winners or the losers, orthodox or heretics.

Sources and studies

For challenges to the Bauer Thesis, see the discussion in Darrell L. Bock, *The Missing Gospels*, pp. 44–55 and Andreas J. Köstenberger and Michael J. Kruger, *The Heresy of Orthodoxy*, pp. 23–40. Bart Ehrman's support for Bauer and the articulation of his term 'proto-orthodoxy' can be found in *Lost Christianities*, pp. 172–80.

Understanding Gnosticism, history's greatest heresy

Gnosticism is the best known of the ancient heresies and is associated, often erroneously, with numerous apocryphal texts. The name derives from *gnosis*, the Greek word for 'knowledge'. This knowledge is of two kinds: the knowledge of the divine that comes from mystical union with God, and the knowledge of oneself that comes from an understanding of the origins of humanity.

Gnosticism seems to have originated in concepts drawn from the works of Plato but combined with dualistic thought from religions of the East. Plato, the famous Greek philosopher, conceived of reality as split into two realms: the immaterial realm of forms and ideas, and the material realm, where matter has been shaped into objects and creatures based on the forms and ideas of the immaterial realm. A desk, for example, has certain

19

typical characteristics – legs, a tabletop, perhaps drawers – but a desk in our world is only a pale imitation of the 'Desk' from the realm of forms, which is far 'deskier' than any desk we can ever see in the world of matter. Both the material and im-material realms are the creation of a being Plato called the Demiurge – from the Greek *demiurgos,* meaning 'craftsman'. Plato also discussed an abstract heavenly deity known as 'the Good', the ultimate principle of the immaterial realm. Unfortunately, Plato never explicitly established the relationship between the Good and the Demiurge. This task was left to his later admirers, the Middle Platonists and the Neo-Platonists, who, in various ways, described the Good as the first god, the ultimate creator of the universe, who operates through the Demiurge. The Platonists also saw aspects of the immaterial and material in each human: we are a combination of an eternal, pre-existent soul and a body created out of matter. The goal of all humans is to live like the philosophers, conquering our passions to devote our time to con-templating the Good, and thereby move beyond the material realm observed by our senses and align our minds with the immaterial realm of ideas.

Christian thinkers eager to compete in the marketplace of ideas sought to add sophistication to their traditions by articulating them using Platonic concepts. Gnostic Christians are distinguished from other Christians by the degree to which they embraced Platonism; orthodox Christians, by contrast, retained a greater hold on Jewish traditions. Tertullian, who converted to Christianity in 197 CE, expressed orthodoxy's position best when he asked, 'What has Athens to do with Jerusalem?' (*Prescription against Heretics,* vii). Gnostic Christianity brought something new to Platonic thought with the introduction of ethical dualism – the separation of good and evil. In Gnostic cosmologies (descriptions of the cosmos), the Good is an indescribable, remote being sepa-rated from the heavenly realm, which is dominated by the evil or misguided Demiurge. The Demiurge uses the essence of the heav-enly realm to create humans and then imprisons them in the horrific earthly realm of matter. Their only rescue is to acquire knowledge of their heavenly origins, transcend the world and achieve union with the Good. Humans are assisted in this by a redeemer figure, someone who is sent by agents of the Good to reveal to humans the path of salvation. In Christian Gnosticism the redeemer is Jesus Christ.

Christian Gnostic cosmogonies detail how Christ was created in the heavens and how later he appeared on earth as Jesus of Nazareth, either as a divine being in ghostly form who only seems human – an understanding of Christ known as Docetism, from the Greek word *dokein* ('to seem' or 'to appear') – or temporarily inhabiting the body of Jesus, who is otherwise a normal human being – this is known as 'adoptionism'. When Christ's mission on earth is finished, he simply rises up to the heavens. The evil humans think him defeated, but they have crucified only his shell, Jesus of Nazareth, or someone else in disguise. The severing of Christ from his humanity leads to a lack of interest by Gnostics in the concept of Christ's one-time resurrection in the flesh and allows for Christ to continually revisit his apostles in ghostly form and deliver new revelations.

The Christian Gnostic Demiurge goes by different names – Saklas ('fool') or Yaldabaoth ('daughter of chaos') – but he is identified as Yahweh, the God of the Jewish Scriptures. He creates humans out of clay, and they are animated by the power of light emanating from the true God beyond the heavens. The Demiurge conspires to keep humans in a state of forgetfulness, unaware of their origins. His efforts are frustrated by agents of the true God, like Christ, who try to come to humans' rescue. Another of these agents in some texts is the snake of the Garden of Eden who entices Adam and Eve to eat from the tree of knowledge; if God in this cosmogony is evil, the Gnostics thought, then the snake must be good. Another hallmark of Christian Gnosticism is rigorous abstinence from worldly pleasures, a practice known as asceticism or Encratism. Gnostics believed the world to be an evil place, so its pleasures – including meat, wine and sex – must be avoided. And sex leads to the production of children which only prolongs the existence of the world; celibacy quickens its end.

Orthodox Christian writers fought the Gnostics by writing lengthy critiques of Gnostic beliefs and practices. These critiques often demonized and mischaracterized their opponents, but the critiques are valuable because, in the course of their refutations, the heresy hunters sometimes also provided excerpts of Gnostic texts. For centuries this was all we knew of Christian Gnostics. But a number of never-before-seen texts were discovered in the nineteenth and twentieth centuries, shedding new light on this lost form of Christianity. We learn from these texts that groups labelled Gnostics by the proto-orthodox rarely identified themselves as such; instead they called themselves Christians. And not all Gnostic groups held the same beliefs and practices. Indeed, 'Gnostic' was sometimes employed by the proto-orthodox as an insult for any form of Christianity that was different from their own. Some modern scholars do the same, though careful reading of the texts often shows that many apocryphal works are far more 'orthodox' in their views than they appear at first glance.

Sources and studies

For a helpful introduction to Gnostic thought and literature, see Birger A. Pearson, *Ancient Gnosticism*. The definition of Gnosticism has been challenged in recent years, further demonstrating that not all groups labelled 'Gnostic' shared the same views and that scholarship on early Christianity continues to be influenced by the untrustworthy descriptions of Gnostics provided by the heresy hunters. For more on the problem of defining Gnosticism, see Michael A. Williams, *Rethinking 'Gnosticism'*, and Karen L. King, *What Is Gnosticism?*

In this first chapter we have looked briefly at several terms important for studying the Christian Apocrypha. In all cases we have seen that the terms must be used with care – what constitutes canon varies over time and space, what is 'true' depends on one's perspective, and what is 'Gnostic' relies, at least to some extent, on the influence of orthodox heresy hunters. It is crucial also to keep in mind that scholars should avoid taking sides in early Christian conflicts over correct doctrine and practice, and, in particular for our purposes, in debates over which texts are to be considered Scripture. The Bible took several centuries to achieve fixed form in the West, and longer still elsewhere, and those who determined which texts to include and which to discard are neither right nor wrong in their decisions. That said, it is tragic when those decisions lead to the destruction of works of literature and the eradication of rival forms of Christianity. But despite the efforts of the 'orthodox' to limit what Christians read, apocryphal texts have survived. We turn next to an examination of how scholars recover and study these texts, and a look at the impact of apocryphal texts and traditions on Christian thought and expression.

2

Studying the Christian Apocrypha

A Christian Apocrypha scholar is part archaeologist, part manuscript hunter, part linguist, part historian and part literary critic. Why? Unlike the canonical texts of the Bible, there are no authoritative versions of apocryphal texts for us to use when conducting research. This is because the copies of apocryphal texts that survive today have great variety in their contents, with stories added or removed, and sections sometimes completely rewritten. Mind you, copies of biblical texts also show variation – it is estimated that there are 300,000 variant readings within the 5,500 complete and partial Greek manuscripts of the New Testament – though the vast majority of these variants are quite insignificant. Given this variety in our copies of the biblical texts, imagine the amount of variation that occurs in copies of non-biblical texts which were not subject to any institutional control over the centuries. So it is vital for Christian Apocrypha scholars to examine all of the available sources – including manuscripts in a variety of languages, as well as art, drama and literature which draw upon stories from the texts – so that the precise contents of a text can be established for all of the time periods and locales in which it is found. Only then can we begin to understand how to interpret each text.

This chapter invites readers into the discipline of text criticism. Some consider this the 'grunt work' of biblical studies. It is a tireless, perhaps tiresome, process of tracking down sources for the texts, meticulously transcribing them, comparing their readings and establishing a critical edition for other scholars to use. Biblical scholars cannot do their work without a Bible that approximates to the form in which it was written. So they are indebted to text criticism, even if they don't want to do the work themselves. Scholars of the Christian Apocrypha tend to do their own text-critical work because often the text they want to work with has not been sufficiently established, either because some of the existing manuscripts and sources have yet to be examined or because the text has never been studied before. That's one of the reasons why studying this literature is so exciting and dynamic; there is always the chance that a new manuscript discovery will transform our understanding of a text and, potentially, even dramatically alter our knowledge of Christian history.

Texts and translations

We begin with a short discussion of languages. In the pages that follow, there will be frequent references to languages – some well known, others unfamiliar to many. So it is best to pause moment-arily to mention the various ancient tongues used in composing the texts and describe how their relationships to other languages led to the various versions of the texts we find in the manuscripts.

Virtually all of the early canonical and non-canonical Christian texts known to us were composed in Greek, the language of literature in the eastern Roman Empire and much of the West in the first three Christian centuries. Aramaic was the spoken language in Palestine in Jesus' day, and Hebrew was the chief written language of the first-century Jews, but if a text was to have an impact on the wider world, it had to be written in Greek. As Christianity moved west, Latin increasingly edged out Greek as the language of the Church and as the common spoken language. By the end of the second century there were numerous Latin versions of biblical texts in circulation – so many that it became imperative to establish an authoritative version of the Bible in Latin (Jerome's Vulgate). Many apocryphal texts also were translated into Latin, though sometimes the texts were much transformed in the process; only a handful of later apocryphal texts were composed in Latin. The Latin versions were in turn translated into the languages of Britain (Irish, Anglo-Saxon) and the Romance languages that developed in continental Europe. In south-eastern Europe, just to the north of Greece, the texts were translated from Greek into Church Slavonic. This was the language of the Slavs who began populating the area in the fifth century. It was given written form in the ninth century by two Greek brothers, Cyril and Methodius.

To the east of Palestine, canonical and non-canonical texts were translated into Syriac. Syriac is a dialect of Aramaic that was once spoken, not only in Palestine, but also in Mesopotamia (modern-day Syria, Iraq and south-east Turkey). The centre of Syriac-speaking Christianity was Edessa (now Urfa in south-east Turkey), a city featured prominently in one of the earliest apocryphal texts written in Syriac: the *Abgar Correspondence*. Texts in Syriac and Greek travelled north to Armenia. The Armenian alphabet was created by Mesrop Mashtots (361/372–440) expressly to translate the Bible into the vernacular. Other texts soon followed, including the *Armenian Gospel of the Infancy*. To the north of Armenia, between the Black Sea and the Caspian Sea, is Georgia. Christianity was introduced there in the middle of the fourth century, and Christian literature entered the vernacular – from Greek, Syriac and Armenian – thanks again to the efforts of St Mesrop, who created the Georgian alphabet. Syriac texts penetrated also the Arabian peninsula, influencing the early development of Islam. Stories from the apocryphal infancy gospels even appear in the Qur'an, likely via Syriac translations, even if in oral, rather than written, form. With the Arab invasion of Egypt, Palestine and Mesopotamia, Arabic became the dominant spoken language, but because its written form was still in development, Arabic was written using Syriac letters. This combination of Arabic and Syriac is known as Garshuni (or Karshuni). Some apocryphal texts, like the *Life of John the Baptist by Serapion*, survive only in Garshuni.

In Egypt, the local language was written in the Coptic script – a combination of 24 Greek letters and seven additional signs to express sounds not in spoken Greek – from as early as the third century. Knowledge of Coptic became very important for the study of the Christian Apocrypha with the discovery of the Nag Hammadi Library in 1945. This fourth-century collection contains our only complete copy of the *Gospel of Thomas* and over a dozen other apocryphal texts. To the south of Egypt and across the Red Sea from the western tip of the Arabian Peninsula is Ethiopia. The origins of Christianity in Ethiopia are mysterious, but it seems to have reached the region in the fourth century and grew vigorously in the fifth and sixth centuries due to the efforts of missionary activity from Egypt and Syria. At first, texts were translated in Ethiopia directly from Greek into Ethiopian, using a script known as Ge'ez. But after the thirteenth century, Greek, Syriac and Coptic texts were translated instead from Arabic. The popular Ethiopic *Miracles of Jesus*, for example, is a translation of the apocryphal Arabic *Gospel of John*, a tenth-/eleventh-century compilation of earlier texts originally composed in Greek (the *Protevangelium of James*, the *Acts of Pilate*, and others).

It is not uncommon for an apocryphal text to have survived in a number of ancient languages. Scholars hope to find copies of the texts in Greek (usually their language of origin), but sometimes the texts are better preserved in languages from more remote regions, like Ethiopia or Iraq. Command of one ancient language is difficult enough to achieve, never mind several. But the more languages a scholar knows, the better he or she is equipped to work on the texts.

Sources and studies

For more extensive discussion of the ancient translations of Christian texts, see Bruce Metzger's *The Bible in Translation*.

Buried treasures

If the Christian Apocrypha were suppressed by orthodox Christianity, where do the texts we study come from? For early copies of apocryphal texts, we rely primarily on happenstance discoveries of texts hidden away in caves, buried in cemeteries or thrown on garbage heaps. In arid climates, like Egypt or southern Israel, texts survive the passage of time with little decomposition or damage. For example, the Dead Sea Scrolls, a major archive of biblical and non-biblical Jewish texts, were placed in jars in caves overlooking the Dead Sea in the first century and there they remained until they were found in 1947.

In many cases, we do not know where manuscripts of our texts come from – they just appear on the antiquities market, presumably discovered by grave robbers, stolen from archaeological sites or happened upon by Bedouin peasants. Consider the case of the second-century manuscript of the unknown gospel of Papyrus Egerton 2. The manuscript was purchased from a dealer in Egypt in 1934; nobody knows anything more about its origins.

Scholars much prefer to work with texts found under the watchful eyes of archaeologists. A text found *in situ* – that is, one that has not been removed from its original place of deposition – is much easier to date and authenticate. For example, a sixth-century book containing fragments of the *Gospel of Peter* and the *Apocalypse of Peter* was found by archaeologists in a monk's grave in Akhmim in Upper Egypt. Finding the book with its owner verifies that it is a true ancient text, not a forgery, and tells us that the texts within it, though explicitly declared apocryphal in the fourth century, were nevertheless valued by an Egyptian monk a few centuries later.

Oxyrhynchus Papyri and the Dishnā Papers

Archaeologists found several other apocryphal texts in the remains of the ancient city of Oxyrhynchus, located 180 kilometres southeast of Cairo. In the time of Jesus Oxyrhynchus was a prosperous Greek town. In medieval times it contained numerous churches and monasteries, reputedly housing 10,000 monks and 20,000 nuns, but by the thirteenth century it had fallen into decline and was abandoned. When the British began excavating Egypt in the late nineteenth century, they did not hold out much hope that Oxyrhynchus would yield anything of great value. But in 1897 excavators B. P. Grenfell and A. S. Hunt found the garbage dumps of the ancient city, and buried within them were thousands of pages of papyrus dating from the first to the sixth centuries. The publication of the papyri, the majority of them now housed at the Ashmolean Museum in Oxford, began in 1898 and continues to today. Ninety per cent of the material is documentary evidence – letters, receipts, etc. revealing much about life in the ancient city – and the remaining 10 per cent is literature, including classical works, Jewish and Christian biblical texts, and several very interesting apocryphal writings. The best known of these consists of three pages from three separate copies of the *Gospel of Thomas* (P.Oxy. 1, 654 and 655) dated to the second and third centuries. Oxyrhynchus also gave us very early fragments of the *Gospel of Mary* (P.Oxy. 3525), the *Acts of Peter* (849), the

Acts of Paul (6), the *Acts of John* (850), the *Protevangelium of James* (3524), perhaps the *Gospel of Peter* (2949, 4009), and several unidentified gospels (210, 840, 1081, 1224).

Travel another 300 kilometres south along the Nile River and you find the town of Dishnā. In 1952, just 5 kilometres away from the town, two peasants searching for fertilizer found a jar containing ancient texts. Some of the texts were in bad condition and were burned on the spot, some were given away to passers-by, and one was even used as tinder to light a water pipe. The bulk of those that survived were sold through intermediaries to the Bodmer Library in Geneva, some went to the Chester Beatty Library in Dublin, and the remainder ended up in seven other locations. Today the manuscripts are known as the Dishnā Papers or, less accurately, the Bodmer Papyri. The find includes 32 ancient books in Greek, Coptic and Latin. They date from the third to the fifth centuries and include Christian, Jewish and classical works (including Homer, Menander and Cicero). Also found in the jar were copies of correspondence by Pachomius (*c.* 290–346), the founder of the first monastic order in Upper Egypt, as well as other letters and texts related to the order. Likely, then, these manuscripts originally belonged to a monastery that would have overlooked the cliff where the texts were found. Publication of the Dishnā Papers began in 1954, and some remain unpublished today. They include a complete manuscript of the *Protevangelium of James* (P.Bodmer V; Greek; fourth century), a copy of the apocryphal correspondence between Paul and the Corinthians (P.Bodmer X; Greek; fourth century), and a story from the *Acts of Paul* (P.Bodmer XLI; Coptic; fourth century).

The presence of both canonical and apocryphal Christian texts among the Oxyrhynchus Papyri and the Dishnā Papers illustrates the range of texts available to and used by Christians up to at least the fourth century. Looking at the number of early manuscripts found in Egypt, Helmut Koester, a renowned Christian Apocrypha scholar from Harvard Divinity School, noted that the physical evidence for early Christian gospels indicates that non-canonical texts were just as popular as those that became canonical. This is because papyri dating from 100 to 300 CE are equally balanced between canonical and non-canonical gospels.

Of course, the number of papyri may not be the best way to assess the popularity of these texts, especially considering that the pool of material is small and limited geographically to a few scattered locations in Egypt, but Koester helps to make the point that, in the early centuries, Christians were exposed to a wide assortment of texts about Jesus and his followers, and only later were some of these declared authoritative.

The Nag Hammadi Library

By far the most famous discovery of apocryphal Christian texts is the collection of writings known as the Nag Hammadi Library. Just 12 kilometres away from the discovery of the Dishnā Papers, another pair of peasants looking for fertilizer found another cache of texts in another jar. It was 1945 when Muhammad Ali al-Samman and his brother broke open this jar and found 12 codices (the Latin word for 'books') and part of a thirteenth. Muhammad brought the codices home, where some of one book was burned by his mother out of superstitious fear of its contents. Eventually the texts came into the hands of dealers and finally to the attention of scholars. They became known as the Nag Hammadi Library after the name of the town located 10 kilometres from the find. The 13 codices are written in Coptic and were created around 350 CE, though the texts within the books were certainly written earlier and likely were all translated from Greek.

In total, the codices of the Nag Hammadi Library contain 52 separate texts, six of which are duplicates (the *Apocryphon of John*, for example, occurs three times). This duplication indicates that the library is a collection of several smaller libraries, perhaps three in total. Like the Dishnā Papers, the Nag Hammadi Library may have belonged originally to monks from a nearby monastery – though, in this case, none of the texts are canonical and they may have been hidden away in fear of reprisal from Church officials enforcing the newly formed canon promoted by Athanasius. All of the texts share an interest in a kind of esoteric mysticism often associated with Gnosticism, but not all of them originated in Gnostic circles. The fragment of Plato's *Republic*, for example, predates Christian Gnosticism by at least four centuries. Only 15 of the texts can be considered Christian Apocrypha; they include the *Gospel of Thomas*, the *Gospel of Philip*, the *Dialogue of the Saviour* and several apocalypses (of Peter, of James and of Paul). Other texts, such as the *Treatise on the Resurrection* and the *Gospel of Truth*, are treatises composed by members of second- or third-century theological schools. And others are not Christian at all, like *Allogenes* and the *Discourse on the Eighth and Ninth*. The manuscripts of the Nag Hammadi Library are now housed in the Coptic Museum in Old Cairo. Their publication began in 1956. These initial efforts were followed by a multi-volume facsimile edition in 1972–7, and then a widely available English translation of the entire corpus.

Additional manuscripts

Several other manuscripts with contents similar to the Nag Hammadi find but of unknown origins have also made their way to scholars through intermediaries. The third-century Coptic Askew Codex – named for its one-time owner, the English physician Dr Anthony Askew – contains two dialogues between the risen Jesus and his disciples: the *Pistis Sophia* and an unnamed text. The Bruce Codex, also in Coptic but of uncertain date, was named for its owner James Bruce, and contains the two *Books of Jeu* and another unnamed text. And the fifth-century Berlin Codex (P. Berolinensis 8502.1), again in Coptic, contains our largest fragment of the *Gospel of Mary*, another copy of the *Apocryphon of John*, the *Sophia of Jesus Christ* and a single *Act of Peter* believed to be part of the original *Acts of Peter*.

Recently, yet another early Coptic manuscript has come to light, this one containing one of the most extraordinary ancient gospels: the *Gospel of Judas*. The manuscript, along with two other ancient books, was found in 1978 by looters of a tomb 60 kilometres north of the town of Al Minya (246 kilometres south of Cairo). It came into the hands of dealers who, aware of the value of finds like the Nag Hammadi Library, tried for decades to sell it for a large sum of money. As the years passed, the codex became increasingly damaged. Finally, it was purchased by art dealer Frieda Nussberger-Tchacos in 2000. Under her care it was restored and published in 2007. In recognition of her work, the manuscript has been named Codex Tchacos. Some additional fragments of the manuscript were held back from the sale but have been recovered and are in the process of being published. Along with the *Gospel of Judas*, the manuscript contains the *Letter of Peter to Philip* and the *First Revelation of James* (both of which are found also in the Nag Hammadi codices), and a new, unnamed text featuring the figure Allogenes.

All of these once-buried treasures present us with ideal sources: manuscripts of texts close in time to their composition and, in some cases, even in their original languages. Of course, many of them have suffered damage – so much that we don't even know some of the names of the texts; but the fact that these manuscripts have survived at all is amazing. The discoveries also demonstrate shifting attitudes to this literature over time. In second- and third-century Egypt, canonical and non-canonical texts sat side by side in libraries or personal collections; but by the fourth century, apocryphal texts had to be hidden from the authorities seeking to destroy them. Nevertheless, some apocryphal material continued to be valued, so much that, even centuries later, monks were buried with books that contained cherished but forbidden texts.

Sources and studies

For more information on Oxyrhynchus, see Peter Parsons, *City of the Sharp-nosed Fish*; on the Dishnā Papers see James Robinson, *The Story of the Bodmer Papyri*. The discovery of Codex Tchacos is narrated in Herbert Krosney, *The Lost Gospel of Judas*. The Nag Hammadi Library was initially published in English by James Robinson; his edition has been superseded by the international edition of Marvin Meyer, *The Nag Hammadi Scriptures*. Helmut Koester's discussion on canonical and non-canonical papyri is from his article 'Apocryphal and Canonical Gospels'.

Monastic libraries

Despite the Church's insistence that non-canonical texts should be avoided or, at worst, destroyed, many of them continued to be copied and treasured in monasteries, the centres of literary production in medieval times. Biblical, apocryphal and even pagan texts shared shelf space in the monastery libraries, sometimes even side by side in individual manuscripts. Monasteries rarely possess manuscripts as early as those found in archaeological sites; the bulk of the holdings date from the tenth to the fifteenth centuries, with some produced after the invention of the printing press – even as late as the twentieth century in remote areas.

Scholars became interested in manuscripts of the Christian Apocrypha in the fifteenth century with the beginnings of Renaissance humanism, a movement typified by its interest in the study of classical works. The humanists followed the principle of *ad fontes* – going 'back to the sources' – and sought out manuscripts of lost works by patristic and classical authors. These manuscripts became more plentiful after the fall of the Byzantine Empire to the Turks in 1453. Italy was then flooded with Greek Orthodox refugees who brought with them texts previously unavailable in the Latin West. Before long, the humanists turned their attention to the Bible, with Erasmus (1466–1536), the famous Renaissance humanist, leading the charge to use the increasingly available Greek manuscripts to assemble a New Testament in its original language, rather than the Latin of Jerome's Vulgate. Also contributing to the move to examine the origins of the Bible were the Protestants of the sixteenth century who likewise sought to go 'back to the sources' with their notion of *sola scriptura* ('by Scripture alone'), which emphasizes the authority of the Bible over tradition and the will of the Church hierarchy. The humanists' curiosity for manuscripts of ancient literature and the Protestants' challenge to the authority of the Church both kindled an interest in rediscovering the lost texts of the Christian Apocrypha.

One of the first texts to benefit from the spirit of this age is the *Protevangelium of James*. In the early sixteenth century, the French Catholic humanist Guillaume Postel (1510–81) journeyed to Constantinople on a diplomatic mission for his king. While there he was also to gather interesting manuscripts for the royal library. Among the texts he brought back to France was one which he named the *Protevangelium Jacobi* (or 'Proto-gospel of James'; the name 'Jacobi' is often rendered as 'James' in English). When published in 1552, the gospel caused quite a sensation. Postel believed that *James* was the source of the canonical infancy traditions in Matthew and Luke. Protestant writers, meanwhile, used the text to argue for the abandonment of aspects of devotion to the Virgin Mary that, though entrenched in Catholic tradition, seemed at the time to have originated in this apocryphal gospel. Similar arguments, either for the primacy of apocryphal texts or for the non-biblical origins of doctrine, attended the publication of other discoveries, like the *Dormition of Mary* and the *Gospel of Nicodemus*. In the decades immediately before and after Postel's *Protevangelium Jacobi* other texts were haphazardly published in *incunabula* – the term for early printed books. A popular choice for incunabula was the *Gospel of Nicodemus*, which appeared in at least four editions before 1500, and another five in the early sixteenth century. The *Gospel of Pseudo-Matthew*, the *Life of Judas* and the *Epistle of Lentulus* also were published as incunabula.

The transition from the devotional incunabula and haphazardly published manuscript discoveries to the proper scholarly study of the texts was a slow one. The first significant collection of all the previously published texts appeared in 1703 with Volume 1 of Johann Albert Fabricius' *Codex apocryphus Novi Testamenti*. But it was another century before scholars began to apply rigorous methodological principles to their work, so that, instead of printing whatever manuscripts were at hand, they gathered more and more manuscripts and compared their readings to determine which ones were likely to be correct.

In their efforts to establish better and better texts with which to work, scholars journeyed to the East in search of new manuscripts. They travelled to remote monasteries in Greece, Palestine, Egypt, Turkey and Persia, and found texts in such languages as Greek, Syriac, Coptic, Arabic, Armenian and Ethiopic. The major libraries of Europe were stocked with their discoveries. One of the best known of the manuscript hunters of the time is Constantin von Tischendorf (1815–74) of the University of Leipzig. The discovery that he is most famous for is the Codex Sinaiticus, a fourth-century biblical manuscript in Greek found at the library of St Catherine's Monastery in the Sinai desert. Tischendorf found also apocryphal texts in his travels and in 1851 began publication of three volumes of critical editions of apocryphal acts (*Acta apostolorum apocrypha*, 1851), gospels (*Evangelia apocrypha*, 1853) and apocalypses (*Apocalypses apocryphae*, 1866). Like his work on the Bible, Tischendorf's Christian Apocrypha collections are well regarded because of his efforts to use the best and earliest manuscripts to establish as close as possible the original form of each text. Some of his editions of texts remain influential today. Other scholars journeyed to St Catherine's in subsequent years, and the library, second only to the Vatican for the number of manuscripts it contains, yielded more treasures.

Another important eastern source of manuscripts of apocryphal texts is the White Monastery near Sohag in Upper Egypt. The monastery, named for the colour of its walls, was founded in 442. It flourished under the guidance of its second abbot, Shenouda, who initiated a literacy campaign that required all the monks to read and also encouraged skills in manuscript writing. The monastery became one of the greatest libraries in Christian Egypt. After the Arab invasion of Egypt in the seventh century, the monastery began a slow decline but survives today. However, the contents of its library were sold or burgled in the eighteenth and nineteenth centuries. The manuscripts are now scattered all over the world; many of them are dismembered, so that pages from a single manuscript are now held in multiple libraries or museums. This makes identification of the texts difficult, particularly if the pages lack titles. But efforts are underway to reunite the pages, at least virtually, using photographs and digital images. Among the apocryphal works originating from the monastery are Coptic versions of the *Book of Bartholomew*, the *Acts of Thomas*, the *Acts of Paul*, the *Gospel of Nicodemus*, the *Life of Mary*, the *History of Joseph the Carpenter*, and several unidentified texts, as well as chronicles and homilies that incorporate apocryphal traditions.

St Catherine's and the White Monastery are not the only libraries of the East. Collections are found in monasteries and churches in Turkey, Iran, Iraq and Armenia, as well as other locations in Israel and Egypt. Greece, too, has a number of monasteries. The peninsula of Mount Athos, for example, is home to 20 monasteries, each with its own library containing biblical and non-biblical texts. The bulk of these locations have been catalogued, some of the manuscripts have been removed for preservation, and others have been photographed so that they can be made available to scholars. But new discoveries still occur. Every once in a while, a new source for manuscripts – a tiny church in Iran, a hidden room in a monastery – is catalogued, and texts once believed lost for ever are recovered.

Sources and studies

For the career of Constantin von Tischendorf and his dealings with St Catherine's Monastery, see James Bentley, *Secrets of Mount Sinai*. Also of interest are the discoveries made by the twins Agnes Lewis and Margaret Dunlop Gibson, whose remarkable careers are documented in Janet Soskice's *The Sisters of Sinai*. The incunabula of apocryphal texts have yet to be studied in depth. For a look at those discussed here, see Mary Dzon, 'Cecily Neville and the Apocryphal *Infantia Salvatoris* in the Middle Ages' and Zbigniew Izydorczyk, 'The Unfamiliar *Evangelium Nicodemi*'. A history of the White Monastery and a comprehensive description of its holdings can be found in Tito Orlandi, 'The Library of the Monastery of St. Shenute at Atripe'. Mount Athos is well represented on the internet; but for a print introduction to the monastic history of the peninsula see Graham Speake, *Mount Athos: Renewal in Paradise*.

Manuscript research

Establishing a proper, scholarly critical edition of an apocryphal text is no easy task; it also can be rather time-consuming, particularly if the text is found in numerous manuscripts, more so if the manuscripts come in several ancient languages. Few people outside the field of text criticism understand how critical editions are created. I was forced into it myself when studying the *Infancy Gospel of Thomas*, a text available in a number of different languages (Greek, Syriac, Latin, and others) with many of the manuscripts still unpublished. If I wanted to make any substantial argument about the gospel, I needed to recover the contents of the text as it was written many centuries ago. Before we turn to look at the texts, it is useful to learn something about this process, if for no other reason than to understand that our knowledge of the Christian Apocrypha is only as good as the texts we are able to reconstruct.

)crypha collections, you
pts. Some of these refer-
ntion, for example, of 'a
particularly helpful – but
manuscript by its library
at. syr. 377', for example,
Bibliothèque nationale
signations to track down
t they can read them in

ts, scholars can appeal to
s named for Jean Bolland
at is, a scholar of saints)
magisterial five-volume
rk on the hagiographical
h, branching out into a
(Subsidia Hagiographica)
and catalogues of manu-
r to look up a particular
cient and medieval texts
index focused specifically
yphorum Novi Testamenti
e Corpus Christianorum
with – it is written in
phical references – it is an
ryphal texts and versions

cripts is in hand, the next
ues for more information.
lolars who visited mona-
s of their contents and, in
cripts. These photographs
l libraries. Many libraries
anuscripts, purchased or

pilfered by the library or donated to it by collectors. The catalogues are of varying quality. Some are highly descriptive, providing such important information as the size, date, materials and
condition of the manuscript, as well as a description of scribal
notes and a selection of bibliographical resources for each text.

Some do little else but list the texts in the manuscript. And these lists may not be entirely accurate; sometimes texts are skipped, the date is wrongly assessed or the cataloguer is unaware of the standard titles used for the texts. This can make finding the text you want difficult, but it is also exciting to look in a catalogue for one text and happen upon another that has not been mentioned before. The final step is to obtain a copy of the manuscript, either by making your own in person or by ordering a reproduction. If the manuscript hunting process seems daunting, be comforted that it is becoming easier as more and more libraries are digitizing their collections and making them available online at no cost.

When all of the manuscript copies have been obtained, the researcher must then compare all of the readings and determine which ones best represent the original text. Some apocryphal texts come in a variety of forms, with stories added or omitted, and with considerable variation in vocabulary and sentence structure. These variations allow for the sources to be classified as belonging to a particular version, or 'recension', of the text – often designated by scholars by such terms as 'Greek A', 'Greek B', 'Latin A', 'Latin B', etc. – each varying considerably from the other. Manuscripts within a recension can be divided into families – subgroups of manuscripts sharing particular variant readings. Sometimes these shared variants indicate relationships between the manuscripts, showing, for example, that one manuscript has been copied off another or that both are copies of a now-lost manuscript. Identifying such relationships helps to determine which is the best manuscript of the text. But it's not easy. Manuscripts can be very difficult to read. Because they are copied by hand, copyists sometimes accidentally skip lines or even entire columns of text; they might even add readings from other manuscripts, or omit readings they find offensive. Misspellings also are common, as are abbreviations of words. Some manuscripts show signs of physical, rather than typographical, damage, such as tears, holes and water damage.

The ultimate goal of this process is the creation of a critical edition that reflects, to the best of the scholar's expertise, the text as it was when composed. This original text can be elusive. Often the manuscripts allow only a view of the text as it was known at a particular point in its transmission – even early manuscripts, like the second- and third-century fragments of the *Gospel of Thomas*, may not represent the text exactly as the author wrote it; so imagine how far a text in a manuscript from the eleventh century has strayed from the original. Some scholars discourage making claims about the contents of the original text, since it is impossible to know what it contained, and advocate instead examining the text in its various forms in their recoverable contexts – for example, an eleventh-century version of the *Gospel of Pseudo-Matthew* as an expression of eleventh-century devotion to Mary. No matter where you stand on this issue, it must be remembered that any conclusions made about the original contents of the texts can only be tentative. It can be embarrassing to produce a study of a text only to have another scholar later discover a much-different manuscript of the text that appears to be closer to its original form.

Sources and studies

François Bovon offers an excellent guide to manuscript research in his essay 'Editing the Apocryphal Acts of the Apostles'. For more on the Bollandists, visit their website at <www.kbr.be/~socboll/index.php>.

Apocrypha in art, literature and drama

Art

Though Athanasius and other Church writers commanded Christians to reject and even destroy the Christian Apocrypha, the texts continued to have a significant influence on Christians through images on sarcophagi and in manuscripts, paintings, icons and church decoration. Knowledge of these images can be helpful for dating apocryphal texts and for determining where they were valued. In the Swiss village of Zillis, for example, visitors to the church of St Martin can still look up to the church ceiling to see eleventh-century scenes of Jesus' childhood drawn from the *Gospel of Pseudo-Matthew*. Apocryphal infancy gospels also contribute to the cycle of stories about Mary in the Scrovegni Chapel in Padua, Italy, decorated by Giotto in 1304–5. Scenes of Mary's death from the *Dormition of Mary* are particularly widespread. Early examples of these are found in ninth-century frescoes in the Church of Santa Maria Egiziaca in Rome and the Church of Agac Alti in Cappadocia.

The importance of images is observable also in the eastern Christian veneration of icons – hand-painted portraits of the holy family, saints and angels, and depictions of biblical stories. These adorn both churches and homes. One particularly noteworthy icon from St Catherine's Monastery on Mount Sinai features four scenes from a triptych of the story of the Abgar Legend from the *Doctrine of Addai*. In one panel, King Abgar holds the portrait of Jesus painted for him by his messenger Hannan. Copies of this portrait, called the Mandylion, were extremely popular in the Middle Ages.

Given that average Christians in medieval times were illiterate, the images they saw in church and elsewhere would have had a great impact on their knowledge of Jesus, his family, and other early Christian figures. The distinction between canonical and non-canonical traditions was meaningless to them.

Literate Christians would see additional images from the Apocrypha in manuscripts. The richest and most elaborate of these 'illuminations', as they are called, are found in biblical manuscripts, where scenes from the lives of the apostles taken from apocryphal acts decorate the New Testament texts written in their names. For example, the life of the apostle John, drawn from the *Acts of John* and related texts, is the basis for an extensive cycle of scenes in a thirteenth-century manuscript of Revelation from Trinity College in Cambridge. Other biblical manuscripts include images reflecting the story of an apostle's martyrdom, such as the beheading of Paul from the *Acts of Paul*, or the upside-down crucifixion of Peter from the *Acts of Peter*. As for apocryphal texts, some manuscripts feature illuminations directly relating to episodes from the texts. One memorable fourteenth-/fifteenth-century Latin manuscript in the Ambrosian Library (L58 sup.) resembles a child's picture book, with its series of canonical and apocryphal stories about Jesus, each accompanied by a drawing of the scene.

Early images of apocryphal traditions can be helpful in determining the origins and dispersion of texts. The familiar scene of the ox and the ass in the manger at the birth of Jesus is found on a sixth-century sarcophagus lid from Milan. This pre-dates the date assigned to the composition of the *Gospel of Pseudo-Matthew*, the earliest text to feature the scene, by two centuries. Does this mean that the gospel must be dated earlier? Or did the tradition have a life before it was incorporated into the text? Perhaps the situation is even more complex – that apocryphal traditions weaved in and out of texts, oral traditions and art over the centuries. Their precise source may be just as elusive as the 'original text' is for text critics.

Literature

Stories from the Christian Apocrypha occasionally were given new form in other literature. Homilies – teachings given to a congregation in oral or, if the author is of sufficient esteem, in written form – sometimes feature apocryphal traditions alongside biblical stories. Many of the homilies with apocryphal traditions are anonymous or attributed, whether wilfully or mistakenly, to early Church writers such as John Chrysostom and Cyril of Jerusalem. Some fragmentary texts identified by scholars as apocryphal gospels, such as the *Gospel of the Saviour*, may derive instead from homilies.

Another category of literature that draws upon the Christian Apocrypha is the collections of lives of the saints. The best known of these is *The Golden Legend* compiled by Jacobus de Voragine around 1260. Jacobus was an Italian Dominican monk who went on to become the Archbishop of Genoa; today he is venerated as a saint in the area. His collection follows in the tradition of martyrologies and legendaries – known as *menologia* and *synaxaria* in the East – which list the martyrs and other saints, sometimes with biographical details and stories, in calendar order of their anniversaries or feasts. Two hundred saints are covered in *The Golden Legend*, using material from some 130 sources including the *Nativity of Mary*, the *Gospel of Nicodemus*, the *Life of Judas*, and various apocryphal acts. *The Golden Legend* was immensely popular. One thousand manuscripts survive, and it was widely printed, in its original Latin and in every western European language. It is second only to the Bible as the most widely read book in the Middle Ages.

Apocryphal texts and traditions also turn up in what are called 'chronicles' – chronological accounts of important facts and events through history. Apocryphal traditions, such as the names of the Magi (the three wise men from the Gospel of Matthew), are sometimes used to flesh out the stories. Entire texts can be incorporated also, such as the *Revelation of the Magi*, which is known today only because it was used by the author of the *Chronicle of Zuqnin*, and the *Legend of the Thirty Pieces of Silver*, which is included in Solomon of Basra's *Book of the Bee*.

Drama

The interplay between history and Apocrypha appears again in drama. In medieval Europe, villagers were treated to cycles of 'mystery plays' performed in the streets by members of trade guilds. The plays covered biblical episodes from Creation to the Last Judgement, though the majority of them focused on the life of Jesus. The York Mystery Plays, performed from the fourteenth to the sixteenth centuries in the city of York, included the Descent to Hell from the Pilate Cycle of texts; the N-Town Plays of the fifteenth century also included Pilate Cycle episodes along with several plays drawing material from the *Nativity of Mary* and the *Dormition of Mary*.

Depictions of hell in drama, as well as in art and literature are drawn not from the Bible, which says very little about the netherworld, but from apocryphal apocalypses. The earliest Christian tour of hell, which itself draws on Greek and Jewish traditions, is found in the *Apocalypse of Peter*. Much of its content was subsequently used in the *Apocalypse of Paul*, and from there it entered into popular consciousness. One of the most dramatic, and influential, depictions of hell can be found in *Inferno*, the first book of Dante Alighieri's three-part fourteenth-century epic poem *The Divine Comedy*. The poem may even contain an explicit allusion to Paul's experiences in hell from the *Apocalypse of Paul* in Dante's mention of the 'Chosen Vessel' (a term for Paul in Acts 9.15) who went there (canto 2.28).

This is just a taste of the influence that the Christian Apocrypha have asserted on art, literature and drama in the centuries leading up to the Renaissance. The goal of the overview is to illustrate, once again, that apocryphal texts did not vanish with the solidification of the canon beginning in the fourth century. Yes, some of the more theologically radical texts were lost or hidden away until recently, but many of the texts were continually read, copied, transformed, and also adapted into other media by pious Christians to meet their own needs and the needs of their communities. The Bible alone has never been enough.

Sources and studies

David Cartlidge and J. K. Elliott's *Art and the Christian Apocrypha* provides a comprehensive study of the influence of the Christian Apocrypha on art. For a shorter discussion of the topic, adding also drama and literature, see J. K. Elliott, 'The Non-Canonical Gospels and the New Testament Apocrypha'. Voragine's *The Golden Legend* is available in a two-volume English translation by William Granger Ryan.

We have come to the end of the introductory chapters that form the necessary base for our exploration of the Christian Apocrypha. You now have an understanding of the variety of sources available to us for reconstructing the texts, and an awareness of the impact of the texts on Christian belief and culture over the centuries. You have been introduced also to the process of creating critical editions, and have seen how, despite the importance of these editions, our knowledge of the texts is always tentative, because a new manuscript discovery can radically change our reconstructions of the elusive original text. For more extensive study of the Christian Apocrypha, there is an appendix at the back of this book that provides an overview of the major resources in the field. The contributions made by Christian Apocrypha scholars, particularly the text critics and translators, are so vital; without them there would be no texts for us to read. But read them we can. Just turn the page and the secret scriptures will be revealed.

3

The apocryphal life of Jesus

In the next few chapters we will take brief looks at a large selection of texts from the Christian Apocrypha. Some of these texts may be familiar to you – many readers doubtless know something about the *Gospel of Thomas* or the *Gospel of Judas* – but others will be entirely new, offering shocking stories about such occurrences as the flying head of John the Baptist, the time when Jesus 'spent the night' with a young man, and the apostle Peter's declaration that Paul's views on Jesus are 'lawless and absurd'. Unfortunately, there is not space enough to examine every text. At the last count there are over 300 known apocryphal texts and, to loosely paraphrase the conclusion to the Gospel of John (21.25), there is no book large enough to contain everything Jesus did. If you are interested in reading more about the texts, the 'Sources and studies' boxes at the end of each section provide information on up-to-date English translations and direct you to more expansive studies of topics covered in the summaries. Full information about all of these resources can be found in the bibliography at the back of the book.

The texts are divided for convenience's sake into three groups. The first covers the life of Jesus from his birth to the end of his preaching career; these texts are usually called 'gospels', though they sometimes differ considerably in form from the biographical Gospels found in the New Testament. The second group contains texts about Jesus' death and resurrection; many of these are dialogues in which the risen Jesus answers questions posed to him by his disciples. And the third group focuses on what happened to Jesus' family and followers after his Ascension to heaven; some of these texts are similar to the canonical Acts of the Apostles, though instead of describing the activities of the apostles working as a group, apocryphal acts document the careers of individual apostles.

The New Testament Gospels offer us only a glimpse at the life of Jesus. Mark and John focus on his adult career. Matthew and Luke expand the story with infancy narratives covering Jesus' birth, infancy and childhood. But so much remains untold. Doubtless this is one of the reasons why other writers saw a need to 'fill in' details about Jesus' life passed over in silence by the canonical Gospels. But not all apocryphal writers felt constrained by the four Evangelists' narratives. Some wrote entirely new gospels telling their own version of Jesus' life and teachings. And it is entirely possible that some of these rival gospels pre-date the other four. Other writers crafted texts that combined stories from a variety of texts about Jesus, thus ignoring distinctions between canonical and non-canonical traditions. Not all of the apocryphal gospels have survived. The championing of the four New Testament Gospels led to the suppression, if not destruction, of many of the texts found objectionable to 'orthodox' Christianity. Nevertheless, what survives is indicative of the keen interest shown by Christians in writing, reading and hearing stories of Jesus.

Infancy gospels

The large gaps in the biography of Jesus left by the canonical Gospels are filled, at least in part, by the infancy and childhood traditions found in non-canonical sources. These provide answers to such questions as: who were Mary's parents? Why did the Magi follow the star to Bethlehem? And, what was Jesus like as a child? Very little is said in any non-canonical gospel, however, about Jesus' teen years and his twenties. But that's not so unusual. Ancient biographers operated under the belief that personality was static, that the qualities one held in adulthood were present throughout one's life. When childhood stories are included in ancient biographies, they are employed primarily to make the point that the hero or heroine of the tales displayed signs of future greatness even in youth. Adolescence is portrayed only in biographies of philosophers, who showed their future promise in secondary, not primary, school. So what modern readers may see as a gap in the biographical record, ancient writers saw as a stage of life with little importance for their subject. Note also that the filling of gaps was not motivated merely by curiosity; rather, each story has a specific purpose, whether to clarify theological and Christological issues, to resolve literary contradictions or to respond to the challenges of critics and heretics – all problems occasioned by what is provided or neglected in the infancy narratives of Matthew and Luke.

There are two main non-canonical infancy gospels: the *Protevangelium of James* and the *Infancy Gospel of Thomas*. Both of these were written quite early – around the middle of the second century. They were also very popular. Over the centuries they were transmitted far and wide, translated along the way into a variety of languages, and often combined with other texts and freely circulating stories. Officially, the infancy gospels were banned by the Church (and remain so), but that did not stop them from exerting an influence on art and literature and feeding imaginations hungry for information about Jesus and his family.

The *Protevangelium of James*

What makes Mary of Nazareth a suitable mother to the Son of God? Why is she so special? This is the main question that the *Protevangelium of James* seeks to answer. As we have seen in Chapter 2, when the gospel was first published in the sixteenth century its editor called it the *Protevangelium* (or 'Proto-gospel') *Jacobi*, a fitting title since it begins with events that took place prior to the infancy narratives of the New Testament. Some early commentators even believed it to be a source used by Matthew and Luke. But it appears to have its origins in the mid-second century. Its popularity in antiquity and through to the Renaissance is evident in the large number of sources now available to us, including over 150 Greek manuscripts and sources in Latin, Coptic, Ethiopic, Armenian, Georgian and Slavonic. The earliest manuscript is a complete fourth-century copy of the text in Greek found among the Dishnā Papers (P.Bodmer V) – an incredible find.

The *Protevangelium* is principally a biography of Mary. It begins with her parents, Anna and Joachim, who, though prosperous, suffer the shame of childlessness. Joachim withdraws into the wilderness to confront God with his complaint. In his absence, an angel appears to Anna and promises her she will conceive a child who 'will be spoken of throughout the entire world' (4.1). An angel then appears to Joachim, revealing to him that Anna has conceived – a miraculous conception, given that Anna became pregnant while Joachim was absent. Mary's parents promise the child to the Temple, but for her first few years she is protected at home.

> 'As the Lord my God lives [her mother says], you will not walk at all on this ground until I have taken you up to the Temple of the Lord.' Then she made a sanctuary in her bedroom and did not allow anything impure or unclean to pass through her lips. (6.1)

At three years old Mary is presented to the Temple where she is 'cared for like a dove, receiving her food from the hand of an angel' (8.1). Mary's purity is clearly an important theme in the text. The canonical Gospels establish her as a virgin; *James* adds a copulation-free conception and seclusion from the outside world. Even Mary's food comes directly from heaven.

When Mary reaches the age of 12, the priests say she must leave the Temple 'to keep her from defiling the sanctuary of the Lord' (8.2). She is placed in the care of a reluctant Joseph, here portrayed as an old man with children of his own, including James, the brother of Jesus and fictive author of the text. The gospel then begins to weave in the infancy narratives of Matthew and Luke, resolving the contradictions of these two accounts by harmonizing them into one story. Such harmonization continues to today and is most apparent in the Christmas nativity scenes that feature the angels, shepherds and manger from Luke alongside Matthew's Magi, their gifts and the star they followed to Bethlehem. But *James* does more than combine Matthew and Luke; he adds also elements from other traditions, including locating Jesus' birth in a cave, rather than a stable. And the birth is described in greater detail than in the canonical Gospels:

> They [Joseph and a midwife] stood at the entrance of the cave, and a bright cloud overshadowed it ... Right away the cloud began to depart from the cave, and a great light appeared within, so that their eyes could not bear it. Soon that light began to depart, until an infant could be seen. (19.2)

To be clear here, what *James* is telling us is that Mary gave birth to Jesus supernaturally, without rupturing her hymen; thus she remained a virgin in every respect.

After the visit of the Magi the gospel shifts its focus to John the Baptist, narrating his escape from the slaughter of the infants by Herod the Great. John's mother Elizabeth takes the infant and flees to a mountain which miraculously opens to conceal them (22.3). John's father, Zacharias, is not so fortunate. Herod's soldiers murder him for refusing to reveal the location of his son. Later writers expand on this story and reveal what happened to John in the wilderness. We will look at these texts in Chapter 5.

The *Protevangelium of James* was banned in the West, in part because it contradicts the explanation offered for the siblings of Jesus put forward by Jerome (they were his cousins, not brothers and sisters, nor step-siblings as in *James*), and perhaps also because of the supernatural nature of Jesus' birth (it makes Jesus too super-human for some believers' tastes). Nevertheless, some of its contents became integral features of Christian tradition, including the names of Mary's parents, the doctrine of the Immaculate Conception (not the virgin birth of Jesus, as many erroneously think, but the notion that Mary was untainted by original sin, occasioned in *James* by Mary's own miraculous conception) and the doctrine of the Perpetual Virginity of Mary. All of these well-known elements of Christian tradition are found here, in this apocryphal text! In the East, the land of Greek Orthodoxy, *James* achieved great popularity. There its characterization of James and the other siblings as Joseph's children became accepted, and special feast days were instituted based on events from the narrative, such as the Presentation of Mary in the Temple (celebrated on 21 November).

The *Infancy Gospel of Thomas*

What would happen if the power to change water into wine, calm storms and heal the sick was placed in the hands of a child? According to the *Infancy Gospel of Thomas*, the consequences would be devastating. In this text, Jesus terrorizes the village of Nazareth, maiming and killing his playmates, neighbours and teachers. Readers of the text have often wondered why someone would portray Jesus this way, and the gospel has been cited often as an example of the excesses of the non-canonical gospels in comparison to the more dignified stories in the New

Testament Gospels. But read in its appropriate literary context – that is, as an example of ancient biography – *Infancy Thomas* is not so shocking at all.

The *Infancy Gospel of Thomas* is one of the earliest apocryphal Christian texts. Stories from it are mentioned by writers of the late second century, but the text's lack of borrowings from the canonical Gospels suggests it could have been written significantly earlier. Though composed in Greek, the early versions of the text (Syriac, Ethiopic, Latin and Georgian) are better witnesses to its original form, a form that lacks, among other things, the introduction attributing the text to Thomas. So the text appears originally to have been anonymous; its title was simply 'The Childhood of Jesus'.

The gospel covers activities in Jesus' life from the ages of five to 12. It begins with Jesus playing with other children at a stream. Then follows a series of curses: Jesus makes one child wither as punishment for disrupting his play, murders another for bumping into him and blinds some villagers when they criticize him for his misdeeds. These curses lead to the text's main act: an episode stretching over three chapters (chs 6—8) in which a teacher named Zacchaeus tries to correct Jesus' behaviour through education. But Jesus outwits the teacher, stupefying him with a speech in which he promises to offer a teaching 'that no-one else knows nor is able to teach' (6.2b). Humbled by Jesus, Zacchaeus delivers a lengthy lamentation, declaring that Jesus is

> not of this world . . . maybe he was born before the world came into being. I cannot fathom what kind of uterus bore him or what kind of womb nourished him . . . What kind of great thing he could be – whether a divine being or an angel – I do not know even what to say. (7.2,4)

Appeased, Jesus then restores those he cursed to health.

The episode of Zacchaeus finished, we now see the theme of the text: each miracle, whether a blessing or a curse, is a demonstration of Jesus' divine origins. He does not need to be disciplined or taught; rather it is the townspeople (or the world) who have a lesson to learn: that Jesus is some 'kind of great thing' (7.4). The text continues with a few beneficent miracles – including the resurrection of a dead child and stretching a wooden beam for his father – and two more episodes with teachers, before concluding with a retelling of Luke's story of the 12-year-old Jesus in the Temple.

Whatever the text's theme, it is still difficult for many Christian readers to reconcile the cursing Jesus of the infancy gospel with what they think of as the loving Jesus of the canonical Gospels. So why does *Infancy Thomas* portray Jesus in this way? Ancient biography provides the answer. Ancient writers typically depict their young subjects as miniature adults, not children. They act with maturity and speak with a wisdom that belies their youth. Thus the five-year-old Jesus can dazzle his teachers with his knowledge and deliver mystifying speeches. And given ancient biography's other main motif – foreshadowing the future career of the protagonist – Jesus' cursing in the infancy gospel must be consistent with the writer's views of the adult Jesus. To the author of *Thomas*, Jesus is a holy man in the style of the Jewish prophets Elijah and Elisha who also manifested the power of God to bless and to curse. And the canonical Gospels do hint at a Jesus who curses: he pronounces woes on the cities of Chorazin and Bethsaida (Matt. 11.21 / Luke 10.13), withers a fig tree (Mark 11.12–25 / Matt. 21:18–22), and in Luke balances his beatitudes ('Blessed are you who are poor . . .') with a number of woes ('But woe to you who are rich . . .'; Luke 6.20–26).

Early writers who commented on the *Infancy Gospel of Thomas* objected not to its cursing stories but to how its childhood miracles contradict John 2.11, which states that Jesus' first miracle was the transformation of water to wine in Cana. But, in time, some readers did find the curses distasteful and made changes to the text, including the addition of three new episodes – healings/resuscitations of a house builder, a young man and a baby (chs 10, 17 and 18) – very similar in structure to miracles in the canonical Gospels. The young Jesus becomes more like his adult counterpart, but no amount of *blessing* stories can make the reader forget the disturbing tales of Jesus *cursing* his neighbours.

Tales of the Magi

Christians have ever been fascinated with the mysterious Magi who, Matthew tells us, followed a star to bring gifts to the Christ-child.

Numerous efforts were made by writers of the Christian Apocrypha to add more to the story of the Magi. According to the *Legend of Aphroditianus*, found in a number of languages (Greek, Slavonic, Romanian and Armenian) but likely originating in the fifth century, the statues of gods and goddesses in the Persian temple of Juno fell on their faces when the star appeared before them. The Magi follow the star to Bethlehem where they meet Mary, the mother of Jesus. In their own words, they give us our only description of Mary: 'She had long hands, and a body somewhat delicate; and her colour was like that of ripe wheat; and she was round of face, and had her hair bound up.' Luckily the Magi have a servant with them who is 'skilled in painting from life', and they are able to bring back with them an image of both mother and child, which they place in Juno's temple.

By far the longest expansion of the Magi story is found in the *Revelation of the Magi*, which today exists in an eighth-century Syriac manuscript of the *Chronicle of Zuqnin* at the Vatican Library. The *Revelation*'s most recent editor believes the text to have been composed in the second or third century. The story is told from the perspective of the Magi, who reveal details about themselves that differ considerably from what is known of them from other apocryphal traditions. The Magi are usually portrayed as a group of three Persian astrologers or Zoroastrian priests, the number corresponding, presumably, to the three gifts of gold, frankincense and myrrh. They are often named Balthazar, Caspar and Melchior. In the *Revelation*, however, there are 12 Magi, they hail from a mythological eastern land named Shir, and the name 'Magi', it is said, derives etymologically from their practice of praying in silence. They know to follow the star to Bethlehem because they are descendants of Seth, the third child of Adam and Eve, who passed on to them a prophecy told to Seth by his father Adam. Another interesting feature of the text is its ecumenism: all previously known religious expressions, such as Zoroastrianism, are said to originate from the revelation of Jesus Christ. The star, who is also Jesus, tells the Magi,

> I am everywhere, because I am a ray of light whose light has shone in this world from the majesty of my Father, who has sent me to fulfill everything that was spoken about me in the entire world and

in every land by unspeakable mysteries, and to accomplish the commandment of my glorious Father, who by the prophets preached about me to the contentious house, in the same way as for you, as befits your faith, it was revealed to you about me.   (13.10)

Collections of infancy gospels

As the popularity of the early infancy gospels increased, efforts were made to combine the tales into comprehensive accounts of Jesus' early years. The best known of these is a seventh-/eighth-century Latin translation of the *Protevangelium of James* known as the *Gospel of Pseudo-Matthew*. Here the story of the death of Zacharias is replaced with additional stories of Jesus and his parents on their journey to Egypt. Over time, *Pseudo-Matthew* was expanded even further, with stories added from other texts, including *Infancy Thomas* and a lost text referred to by scholars as the *J Composition* (which shares some information with the *Revelation of the Magi*). *Pseudo-Matthew* was immensely popular in the West. The surviving manuscripts number almost 200, and translations exist in a number of other languages including German, French, Danish, Welsh and Anglo-Saxon. It is via *Pseudo-Matthew*, and a later abbreviation known as the *Nativity of Mary*, that apocryphal tales of Jesus' infancy and childhood entered into western art, literature and popular devotion.

Eastern Christians also valued infancy traditions and similarly worked to join together texts about Jesus' early years. One of these is the Syriac *Life of the Blessed Virgin Mary*, which seems to have originated in the fifth century; it is best known in an Arabic translation that scholars call the *Arabic Gospel of the Infancy*. Both forms of the text were quite popular and have left a plentiful manuscript base. The *Life of Mary* is an expansion, like *Pseudo-Matthew*, of the *Protevangelium of James*, but in its present form it includes several other texts and traditions; some manuscripts even add a number of chapters from the *Infancy Gospel of Thomas*. In the tales not found in *James* or *Thomas*, Jesus is still an infant; the healings and exorcisms that occur involve the application of the baby's bathwater or swaddling bands. Several of the stories have the young Jesus encounter figures from later in his life, such as the apostles Thomas and Simon the Zealot, who are healed of illnesses, and Judas, who is freed from the clutches of a demon, but not before he strikes Jesus on his side, precisely where he will be pierced by a spear during the crucifixion.

The collection finishes with a handful of childhood miracles, including a tale of Jesus meeting a dyer, one where Jesus transforms his playmates into goats, and another in which children role-play and make Jesus their king. These three stories sometimes appear in manuscripts of the other infancy gospels, including yet another collection known as the *Armenian Gospel of the Infancy*. This rarely studied text is believed to be a sixth-century translation of a lost Syriac original. Like the *Life of Mary*, it expands the *Protevangelium of James* with additional childhood stories in Egypt and in various locations in and around Galilee. Particularly memorable is the gospel's detailed discussion of the Magi (ch. 11), which shows some contact with the *Revelation of the Magi* traditions, particularly in its discussion of the prophetic text passed on to them by Adam's son Seth (11.23).

Infancy gospels comprise one of the largest categories of the Christian Apocrypha. Certainly this is due to the gaps left by the canonical Gospels that yearn to be filled. But we have also seen how these texts function to establish or promote points of doctrine, such as Mary's post-partum virginity, as well as to solve such riddles as the origins of the mysterious Magi. Less obvious a reason for their creation is simply to satisfy the needs of Christians devoted to the worship and adoration of Jesus and his family – needs evidently not fully met by the officially sanctioned Scriptures.

Sources and studies

All the infancy texts, unless otherwise noted, are quoted from Bart Ehrman and Zlatko Plešе, *The Apocryphal Gospels*. The *Revelation of the Magi* was published recently in its first English translation by Brent Landau. The earliest mention of the names of the Magi is in the *Excerpta Latina Barbari*, a Latin translation of a Greek chronicle originating in the sixth century. The Syriac *Life of the Blessed Virgin Mary* can be read in the edition by Ernest A. W. Budge; the most accessible source for the *Arabic Gospel of the Infancy* and the *Legend of Aphroditianus* is online at the 'New Advent' site; and the *Armenian Gospel of the Infancy* can be read in the new English translation by Abraham Terian. Many of the infancy gospel traditions, including selections from Irish apocrypha, are collected and arranged in chronological order in J. K. Elliott's *Synopsis of the Apocryphal Nativity and Infancy Narratives*.

Ministry gospels

Only a few non-canonical gospels entirely retell Jesus' adult career. It seems that the canonical Gospels were held in such high regard from an early date that most writers felt content to harmonize the canonical texts into one story rather than replace them with competing accounts. Nevertheless, fragments have been recovered of old, otherwise-lost gospels showing us that some Christians conceived of Jesus in ways much different from how he is portrayed in the New Testament. There is reason to believe also that early Christians continued to pass along sayings and stories about Jesus that were available to the canonical Gospel writers but not used in their Gospels. These traditions appear not only in non-canonical gospels but also in works by early Church writers and even in canonical-Gospel manuscripts. This quasi-canonical status – perhaps we could call them 'orthodox apocrypha' – has brought a certain level of esteem to the traditions that is not enjoyed by other apocryphal texts. As a result, scholars are more open to consider them as authentic teachings of Jesus.

Agrapha

Agrapha literally means 'unwritten' and refers to sayings by Jesus that have come down to us through oral transmission – that is, they are preserved in Christian and Muslim sources but are not credited to nor do they appear to have been written down in any particular gospel. Some scholars prefer a more expansive definition of agrapha to include any saying of Jesus not found in the canonical Gospels, thus including material from Acts, the letters of Paul and non-canonical gospels like the *Gospel of Thomas*. This results in a pool of more than 200 sayings, over 400 if Muslim sources are added.

A number of agrapha appear in the sermon known as *2 Clement*, one of the texts of the Apostolic Fathers written at the end of the first century. The anonymous writer quotes nine sayings of Jesus, introduced typically with the formula 'the Lord says'. At least four of these sayings do not appear in the canonical Gospels. For example, when discussing the need to combine faith with actions, the author quotes Jesus as saying,

> Even if you were cuddled up with me next to my breast but did not do what I have commanded, I would cast you away and say to you, 'Leave me! I do not know where you are from, you who do what is lawless.'
> (*2 Clement* 4.5)

The sermon features also an interesting exchange between Jesus and Peter:

> For the Lord said, 'You will be like sheep in the midst of wolves.' But Peter replied to him, 'What if the wolves rip apart the sheep?' Jesus said to Peter, 'After they are dead, the sheep should fear the wolves no longer. So too you: do not fear those who kill you and then can do nothing more to you; but fear the one who, after you die, has the power to cast your body and soul into the hell of fire.'
> (*2 Clement* 5.2–4)

Agrapha appear also in manuscripts of the canonical Gospels. One example occurs in Codex Bezae, an important fifth-century Greek Bible that contains a number of alternate readings in the Gospels and Acts. Here Luke 6.5, 'The Son of Man is lord of the sabbath', is moved later in the text (to 6.10) and is replaced with:

> On the same day, when he saw a certain man working on the Sabbath, he said to him, 'O man, if you know what you are doing, you are blessed; but if you do not know, you are cursed, and a transgressor of the Law.'

Mention should be made also of a number of stories which, though found in select biblical manuscripts, likely were not originally part of the texts. These include the well-known story of the Woman Caught in Adultery in John 7.53—8.11. The story is not found in the oldest and best manuscripts of John; in other manuscripts it is placed after John 21.25, and even shows up in some manuscripts of Luke. Where does this story come from? Another version of the episode was known to Didymus the Blind, a theologian from fourth-century Alexandria who said he read it in a non-canonical gospel. Eusebius, reporting that Papias was aware of the tale, says that it is contained in the *Gospel of the Hebrews* (*Ecclesiastical History* 3.39.17). A note in one manuscript of John (Athos, *Ivéron 56*) reveals that the story is found also in the *Gospel of Thomas*. Another interesting expansion of the Gospels is found in many manuscripts of the Gospel of Luke. The scene is the garden of Gethsemane, just before Jesus' arrest. Jesus implores the Father to 'remove this cup' from him and then the manuscripts add, 'In his anguish he prayed more earnestly, and his sweat became like great drops of blood falling down on the ground' (Luke 22.43–44).

Both of these episodes are examples of apocryphal tales or sayings that entered into the manuscript tradition, perhaps at first in the margins, and over time became part of the texts. The editors of modern Bibles usually place the verses within parentheses and add notes stating that they are not present in the early manuscripts. Nevertheless, some examples of this material, particularly the Woman Caught in Adultery, have become so engrained in Christian consciousness that, despite their origins, they are unlikely to be unseated from canonical status.

Fragments of lost gospels

No complete non-canonical account of Jesus' adult life has yet been found. All we have are fragments of texts, as well as titles and quotations by early Church writers. Efforts have been made to match the fragments with the information provided by the Church writers; but this is difficult, if not impossible, in most cases because none of the fragments include titles. Some of them, such as Papyrus Merton 51 and Papyrus Oxyrhynchus 210 (both of the third century), may not be gospel texts at all, but pieces of harmonies or homilies that contain apocryphal traditions. Nevertheless, the fragments provide us with hints at the existence of otherwise lost gospels, and, given the early date of some of these scraps of text, they show us that non-canonical texts were circulating in the ancient world at the same time as the canonical Gospels – perhaps even earlier!

One of the best-known fragmentary gospel texts is Papyrus Egerton 2, named for the benefactor who facilitated the manuscript's purchase by the British Museum in London. A second fragment, Papyrus Cologne 255, was later determined to be part of the same manuscript. The two scraps have been dated to around 200 CE, making P.Egerton 2 one of our earliest Christian manuscripts. The evidence is small, comprising four pages with text on both sides. Four episodes are preserved. In the first Jesus argues with the 'lawyers' and 'rulers of the people' in exchanges that have echoes in several chapters of John (e.g. 5.39,45; 9.29). The conflict culminates in an attempt to stone Jesus, but he escapes their clutches. He then heals a leper, as he does in similar stories in the Synoptic Gospels (particularly Mark 1.40–44 and its parallels in Matthew and Luke). In the final story Jesus is asked, 'Is it right to pay the kings the things that relate to their rule?', recalling the well-known controversy about paying taxes to Caesar (Mark 12.13–17 and parallels). The fourth episode is entirely new but the damage to the manuscript makes it difficult to read. Jesus stands on the banks of the Jordan and appears to be sowing seeds. P.Egerton 2's combination of Synoptic and Johannine materials is quite curious. Some scholars see it as evidence for a second-century blending of canonical and non-canonical traditions. A few scholars have seen it as evidence that the gospel of P.Egerton 2 pre-dates the canonical Gospels – written in a time before the Johannine and Synoptic traditions became separated.

Another important fragmentary text is found in Papyrus Oxyrhynchus 840. This manuscript is more recent than P.Egerton 2 – it is from the third or fourth century – and the fragment is much smaller: a single leaf measuring only 7.2 by 8.6 centimetres, with writing on the front and back. Scholars think it might have belonged to an amulet or, more likely, a miniature codex. The text features a controversy story occasioned by a challenge to Jesus made by a Pharisee and high priest named Levi. Levi asks Jesus, 'Who has permitted you to trample this sanctuary and to view these holy vessels, when you have not washed nor indeed have your disciples bathed their feet?' Emphasizing inner purity over outward purity, Jesus responds that he and his apostles have washed in the 'waters of eternal life' rather than the pool of David, 'in which dogs and swine have wallowed night and day'. While some have championed P.Oxy. 840 as evidence for an early gospel, the number of historical anachronisms in the text – for example, there is no historical record of a high priest named Levi, and the priests were Sadducees, not Pharisees – along with its clear division between the practices of Christians and Jews suggest that the story comes from a text at some distance from the time and place of Jesus.

The *Gospel of the Saviour*

The most recent discovery of a fragmentary apocryphal gospel is Papyrus Berolinensis 22220, christened the *Gospel of the Saviour* by its editors because of its prevalent use of the title 'Saviour' for Jesus. The manuscript was acquired by the Berlin Egyptian Museum in 1967 but not published until 1999. Since then another fragmentary manuscript, Strasbourg Coptic Papyrus 5–7, published over a century ago, has been identified as containing a portion of the same text. The Berlin fragments are dated to the sixth century, the Strasbourg to around 400. At first it was unclear to the text's editors whether this was a narrative gospel, a dialogue, or a homily with apocryphal traditions. It is now believed that the text was a narrative gospel that was about the same length as the Gospel of Matthew.

The first fragment begins after the last supper, with Jesus in the garden of Gethsemane, teaching his disciples. He predicts his coming betrayal and abandonment by his followers, as in the canonical Gospels. But then he continues with additional teaching occasioned by questions from the apostles, either individually (Andrew is named at one point) or as a group. In the next fragment, the apostles accompany Jesus on a spiritual journey to the throne of the Father: 'We became as [those] among the [immortal] aeons, with our [eyes penetrating all] the heavens, clothed with the [power of] our apostleship, and we saw our Saviour when he had reached the [seventh] heaven' (36). When they return to earth, the apostles ask Jesus about his resurrection. John requests that he return in a different form. 'Do not reveal yourself to us in all your glory,' he says, because they would not be able to bear such a sight (68). Much of the remainder of the available text is a prayer addressing the apostles' concerns about Jesus' coming death. The prayer is interrupted briefly by an address to the cross, in which Jesus says, 'O cross, do not be afraid! I am rich. I will fill you with my wealth. [I] will mount you, O cross. [I] will be [hung] upon you' (104–106). The fragments conclude with a post-resurrection appearance to the apostles.

Two additional sources for the *Gospel of the Saviour* have recently come to light. A Coptic prayer book was discovered containing a 'Hymn to the Cross' that seems to be an excerpt of the address mentioned above. In the prayer book this hymn is preceded by a post-resurrection commission narrative in which Jesus instructs his apostles to go out and preach. The same narrative appears in a text in Old Nubian known in scholarship as the 'Stauros-Text' or the 'Discourse upon the Cross'. The association of the commission narrative with the hymn suggests that the narrative may also be part of the gospel. Also of note is a dedication at the end of the Stauros-Text to 'those who listen to the book of the life-giving cross'. Could this be the original title of the gospel?

The *Gospel of Peter*

Four of the early gospel fragments (P.Oxyrhynchus 2949 and 4009, P.Vindobensis G 2325 and the Akhmim fragment) have been identified by many scholars as excerpts from a *Gospel of Peter* known to early Christian writers. The most significant reference to this gospel is made by Eusebius of Caesarea (*Ecclesiastical History* 6.12.1–6). Discussing Serapion, a second-century bishop of Antioch, Eusebius quotes from a pamphlet written by the bishop called 'The So-called Gospel of Peter'. According to the pamphlet, this *Gospel of Peter* was a narrative gospel about Jesus' adult life that was in use in nearby Rhossus, but it had become controversial because Docetists, Christians who believed that Jesus was not truly human, had made 'spurious additions' to the text. Serapion wrote the pamphlet, not to discourage its use, but to point out these additions to a text that, otherwise, 'accorded with the authentic teaching of the Saviour'.

Serapion's statements were all that was known of the *Gospel of Peter* until the late nineteenth century when a book was discovered in Akhmim in Upper Egypt containing what appears to be a large fragment from this long-lost gospel. The sixth-century book contains a story of Jesus' Passion, burial and resurrection, along with another fragment identified as belonging to the *Apocalypse of Peter* and two other texts. The Passion, from the Latin *patior* ('to suffer'), is a term that encompasses Jesus' arrest, trial, suffering and crucifixion. The canonical Gospels' account of these events, called the Passion Narrative, is one of few areas of overlap in material between John and the Synoptics.

But all four Gospels contain some unique elements – for example, Luke tells us that one of the thieves crucified with Jesus repented of his evil deeds, Matthew reports an earthquake at Jesus' death and mentions guards at his tomb, John includes the mob's demand not to break Jesus' legs, and only in Mark do the women flee from the empty tomb in fear. Strangely, the fragment of the *Gospel of Peter* has all of these features in a single text, along with a number of unique elements of its own. Some of these work to shift the culpability for Jesus' death away from the Romans and place the responsibility solely upon Jesus' fellow Jews. For example, Jesus' trial is presided over by Herod Antipas, not Pilate, and after seeing signs and wonders at Jesus' death, the Jews realize 'the evil they [have] done to themselves' and cry out, 'Woe to us because of our sins. The judgment and the end of Jerusalem are near' (v. 25). The text also contains an account of the resurrection, an event not found in the canonical accounts. In it the guards at the tomb see the skies open and two men descend to earth. Then the stone rolls away from the entrance of the tomb. The guards

> saw three men emerge from the tomb, two of them supporting the other, with a cross following behind them. The heads of the two reached up to the sky, but the head of the one they were leading went up above the skies. And they heard a voice from the skies, 'Have you preached to those who are asleep?' And a reply came from the cross, 'Yes'. (vv. 39–42)

Scholars are divided about how to evaluate the evidence of the *Gospel of Peter*. Most consider it a second-century harmony of the canonical Gospels, though the lack of verbatim agreement with the Gospels suggests that its author composed his text from memory, not rote copying, of the Gospels; this process is often called 'secondary orality'. Another view characterizes the text as a fifth source of the original Passion Narrative. If so, the *Gospel of Peter* would be an independent witness to the same material used by the other Gospel writers and may have preserved some elements of the original source that they did not use.

The *Secret Gospel of Mark*

Scholars have speculated often about the one-time existence of various forms or 'editions' of the canonical Gospels – a Proto-Luke, for example, or an early version of Mark, or a Hebrew Matthew. These theories are weakened by the lack of manuscript evidence for such texts, but we do have some evidence for a longer version of Mark available in second-century Alexandria. Many scholars, however, dispute that evidence, declaring 'longer Mark' a forgery perpetrated by the man who discovered it.

In 1958, as the story goes, North American scholar Morton Smith, while cataloguing manuscripts at the Mar Saba monastery in the Judaean desert, found a copy of a previously unknown letter attributed to Clement of Alexandria (*c.* 150–215). The letter describes a longer version of Mark's Gospel – Clement calls it the 'mystical' or secret gospel – made by Mark himself for the benefit of more intellectually and spiritually gifted readers. Clement's letter is written to a fellow Christian named Theodore who is confused about the contents of *Secret Mark* due to its use by a group called the Carpocratians. According to Clement, their founder, Carpocrates,

> so enslaved a certain presbyter of the church in Alexandria that he got from him a copy of the secret Gospel, which he both interpreted according to his blasphemous and carnal doctrine and, moreover, polluted, mixing with the spotless and holy words utterly shameless lies. (Letter to Theodore 2.4–9)

In his efforts to distinguish Carpocrates' text from the true *Secret Mark*, Clement excerpts two stories, one of which is placed after Mark 10.34 and is similar to the raising of Lazarus from John 11. As in the Lazarus story, a young man has died, and Jesus goes to the tomb and brings him back to life. The young man then becomes enamoured of Jesus and wants to stay at his side:

> But the youth, looking upon him, loved him and began to beseech him that he might be with him . . . And after six days Jesus told him what to do and in the evening the youth comes to him, wearing a linen cloth over his naked body. And he remained with him that night, for Jesus taught him the mystery of the kingdom of God.
>
> (Letter to Theodore 3.4–10)

The Carpocratians apparently made changes to the story, adding, among other things, a reference to 'naked man with naked man' (3.13). Clement's letter continues with a promise to reveal 'the true explanation' (3.18) of the text, but the letter ends mid-sentence, presumably because the copy from which it was made was incomplete.

Many scholars have struggled with the homoeroticism in *Secret Mark*'s depiction of the relationship between Jesus and his young student. The characterization of the text as an anachronistic 'gay gospel' fed assertions made by critics of Morton Smith that the scholar created the text, in part, to test his fellow scholars' ability to detect forgeries. Defenders of the text say *Secret Mark*'s homoeroticism is in the eye of modern readers, not the gospel's author. In an effort to settle the issue, the magazine *Biblical Archaeology Review* commissioned two handwriting analyses of the manuscript. Though the experts disagreed on many points, they both declared that the manuscript was written by a native Greek writer and, therefore, could not be by Smith himself, whose abilities in Greek simply were not strong enough to create the manuscript. This leaves us with several possibilities: that the Letter to Theodore was truly written by Clement of Alexandria and it tells us that there existed a longer version of Mark (written either by Mark himself or someone else), or that the letter is a medieval forgery written in Clement's name, or that it is a product of the seventeenth-/eighteenth-century Greek writer who left the copy of the letter at Mar Saba. Critics of Smith, however, are undaunted by the handwriting analyses and simply have emended their theories of forgery so that Smith must have enlisted someone else to put pen to paper.

Today many scholars still resist working with *Secret Mark*, fearing that evidence will finally present itself proving the text to be a forgery. This stalemate demonstrates how scholars' own sensitivities, biases and even dislike for other scholars can interfere with the study of ancient literature, particularly with gospel texts that describe a Jesus different from the one they know and believe is true to history.

Sources and studies

The gospel fragments and agrapha can be found in Ehrman–Pleše, *The Apocryphal Gospels*, except the *Gospel of the Saviour* and *Secret Mark*; however, both of these are included in Ehrman's *Lost Scriptures*, pp. 52–6 and 87–9. For new developments in the debate over the authenticity of *Secret Mark*, see the essays collected in Tony Burke, *Ancient Gospel or Modern Forgery?* The chief proponent of the theory that the *Gospel of Peter* preserves early Passion Narrative traditions is John Dominic Crossan; his views were articulated first in his book *The Cross That Spoke*. For comprehensive scholarship on the agrapha, see Joachim Jeremias, *Unknown Sayings of Jesus*.

Jewish-Christian gospels

Christianity began as a Jewish movement. Jesus was a Jew, his family were Jews, his disciples were Jews, he preached about the Jewish Torah to Jews in Jewish lands, and the leaders of the Church after his death were Jews, including his brother James. Yet, after Jesus' death, the movement attracted a greater and greater number of non-Jews, thanks largely to the efforts of Paul, the self-appointed apostle to the Gentiles. By the end of the first century the movement had developed its own identity distinct from Judaism – its members became known as Christians. The separation of the two groups became so distinct that, by the fifth century, Jewish Christianity was no longer the norm but a heresy that was soon eradicated. But not before Jewish Christians created some texts of their own which they used as vehicles for their particular views about Jesus and, at times, for attacks against Gentile Christianity.

Jewish-Christian gospels no longer survive except in quotations by early Christian writers and in variant readings noted in the margins of Gospel manuscripts. Despite the fact that we have no full texts available to us, we think the Jewish-Christian gospels were similar to the canonical Gospels in style and structure – that is, they featured narratives and sayings detailing Jesus' life from at least the baptism until his death and resurrection. It is difficult to determine how many Jewish-Christian gospels there were because of the confusion of names in the sources. Most often the citations are assigned to three texts, each named for the group who used it: the *Gospel of the Hebrews,* the *Gospel of the Nazarenes,* and the *Gospel of the Ebionites.* But there is good reason to believe that at least two of the groups used the same text. Jerome, for example, introduces one of his citations by saying, 'In the Gospel which the Nazarenes and the Ebionites use, which we have recently translated out of Hebrew into Greek, and which is called by most people the authentic [Gospel] of Matthew . . .' (*Commentary on Matthew* 12.13).

The *Gospel of the Hebrews,* though eventually declared heretical, is mentioned positively by Clement of Alexandria and his student Origen (*c.* 185–254). The quotations they provide are in Greek, rather than Hebrew as one might expect for Jewish-Christian gospels. Clement's knowledge of the text suggests that it may have been composed in Alexandria around the late first or early second century. The gospel's contents are somewhat esoteric. One excerpt includes an odd reference to the baptism story in which Jesus says, 'Just now my mother, the Holy Spirit, took me by one of my hairs and carried me up to the great mountain, Tabor' (Origen, *Commentary on John* 2.12). But the most interesting of the excerpts features a resurrection appearance to James:

> But when the Lord had given the linen cloth to the servant of the priest, he went and appeared to James. For James had taken a vow not to eat bread from the time he drank the cup of the Lord until he should see him raised from among those who sleep . . . The Lord said, 'Bring a table and bread.' He took the bread and blessed it, broke it, gave it to James the Just, and said to him, 'My brother, eat your bread. For the Son of Man is risen from among those who sleep.' (Jerome, *Illustrious Men* 2)

It is surprising to see James given such a prominent role. The New Testament Gospels and Acts tend to minimize James's contributions to Christianity – he is not listed as one of the apostles, barely appears in Acts, and in the Gospels he is portrayed as antagonistic towards Jesus (John 7.3–5). Yet, according to the *Gospel of the Hebrews*, he was present at the last supper and he spoke to the risen Jesus.

The other Jewish-Christian gospel is said to have been used by the Nazarenes and the Ebionites. 'Nazarene' seems to have been an early name for a follower of Christ and was retained by a Jewish-Christian group living in Syria in the fourth century. Jerome claims they used a Hebrew version of Matthew, though with a number of variations and at least one entirely new story:

> Behold, the mother of the Lord and his brothers were saying to him, 'John the Baptist is baptizing for the remission of sins. Let us go and be baptized by him.' But he replied to them, 'What sin have I committed that I should go to be baptized by him? Unless possibly what I just said was spoken in ignorance.'
>
> (Jerome, *Against the Pelagians* 3.2)

The Ebionites, the other group who used this gospel, have similar origins to the Nazarenes and they resided in the same region. Their name, from a Hebrew word meaning 'poor' or 'oppressed', may derive from the title apparently given to the leaders of the Jerusalem Christian community. In Galatians, Paul recalls being asked by the Jerusalem community to 'remember the poor' (Galatians 2.10), likely a reference to the collection he must bring to Jerusalem (mentioned in 1 Corinthians 16.1–4 and elsewhere) rather than a mandate to care for the impoverished. Irenaeus offers more information on this group. He says they used only the Gospel of Matthew, repudiated Paul and upheld the Jewish law (*Against Heresies* 1.26.2). Elsewhere, he adds that they denied the virgin birth, affirming that Jesus was a son of David through his father Joseph and he was 'adopted' as Messiah at his baptism (*Against Heresies* 5.1.3). Our other principal source for the Ebionites is Epiphanius, the Bishop of Salamis on Cyprus from 366 to 403. Similarly to Irenaeus, he says the Ebionites used a Hebrew version of Matthew, but the seven excerpts Epiphanius provides from the gospel show signs of Greek origin and appear to derive from a harmony of the Synoptic Gospels. It is likely that Epiphanius has confused two texts here. The Ebionites'

Hebrew gospel of Matthew may be the same text as the 'Jewish gospel' (in Greek: *to Ioudaikon*) cited in five manuscripts of the Gospel of Matthew from the ninth to the thirteenth centuries. Two of these citations state that this 'Jewish gospel' was preserved on Mount Zion in Jerusalem.

It is tantalizing to think that the Jewish-Christian gospels may preserve the views of the earliest form of Christianity. Unfortunately, their trail has long run cold. Unless a new manuscript source presents itself, the full content of these texts will remain mysterious.

Sources and studies

The Jewish-Christian gospels are available in Ehrman–Pleše, *The Apocryphal Gospels*. For more detailed study, the primary resource on the texts in English is A. F. J. Klijn, *Jewish-Christian Gospel Tradition*. Readers may be interested also in the recent essay collection *Jewish Believers in Jesus* edited by Oskar Skarsaune and Reidar Hvalvik.

Complete apocryphal gospels

Of all the apocryphal ministry gospels that existed in antiquity, precious few have survived in complete form. And none of these resemble the canonical Gospels. Yes, they report sayings or teachings of Jesus, but there is very little narrative in these texts. It is arguable, also, that the texts are not truly 'ministry' gospels at all because, at times, they appear to be reporting words spoken by Jesus after his resurrection.

The *Gospel of Thomas*

What could be more exciting than discovering an ancient collection of the sayings of Jesus? Particularly if some of those sayings have never been seen before? Excitement did greet the publication of three fragmentary Greek manuscripts from Oxyrhynchus (numbered 1, 654 and 655) at the turn of the nineteenth century. The manuscripts have been dated palaeographically to the second and third centuries – astonishingly early, leaving scholars wondering what that would mean for the date of the composition of the text or texts they contain. Then, in 1945, a text called the *Gospel of Thomas* was found among the Coptic texts of the Nag Hammadi Library and it became clear that the Oxyrhynchus fragments were three separate witnesses to the same text.

The complete *Gospel of Thomas* found at Nag Hammadi is a translation from Greek into Coptic dating to the middle of the fourth century. It features some notable differences from the early Greek fragments, including a shift in the order of the material and both longer and shorter readings. Though the majority of scholarship on the text focuses on the Coptic version, it should be made clear that this version of the gospel is several centuries and one language removed from the original text. Scholars divide the text into 114 individual sayings (known as *logia*). The majority of these are introduced simply with the words 'Jesus said'; the remainder have small amounts of narrative, mostly in the form of a question posed to Jesus by one of his followers. There is no infancy narrative, no miracle stories, no Passion Narrative, no resurrection appearances. Could this mean that these vital aspects of the Jesus story were not important at all to the writer of the text? Some of the sayings in the gospel are quite familiar – such as, 'A prophet is not welcome in his village' (log. 31) and 'Blessed are the poor, for the kingdom of heaven is yours' (log. 54); but some are unique and, at times, even bizarre – such as, 'Blessed is the lion that the human will eat so that the lion becomes human. And cursed is the human who the lion will eat, and the lion will become human' (log. 7) and the enigmatic 'Become passersby' (log. 42).

The *Gospel of Thomas* is often associated with Gnosticism, the form of Christianity we discussed back in Chapter 1. Certainly the text contains some Gnostic elements: salvation comes from 'knowing' one's origins, this knowledge can be found within, and the material world is to be denied. All three of these elements come together in saying 3:

> If your leaders say to you, 'Look, the kingdom is in the sky,' then the birds of the sky will precede you. If they say to you, 'It is in the sea,' then the fish will precede you. But the kingdom is within you, and it is outside you. When you come to know yourselves, then you

will be known, and you will understand that you are children of the living Father. But if you will not know yourselves, then you are in poverty, and it is you who are the poverty.

This idea of salvation independent of religious institutions is attractive to many people today and has contributed to the popularity of the text, particularly among those interested in New Age religions. Less attractive to moderns is the text's promotion of sexual abstinence, evident in its frequent praise of 'the solitary ones' (log. 4, 16, 23, 49, 75), and its doctrine, which involves regaining Eden and the perfect state of the first human, Adam, who had both male and female principles (see log. 18); this can only be done by refusing the command to be fruitful and multiply. Those who argue that *Thomas* is not a Gnostic text cite its lack of typical Gnostic ingredients, such as a detailed Creation myth, and revelations given to readers in a post-resurrection setting (the gospel announces itself as 'the hidden sayings of the living Jesus', which could mean a Jesus who has conquered death, but the context of many of the sayings appears to be Jesus' lifetime).

Also of interest in the text, and similarly ambiguous, is its audience's relationship to Judaism. Many of the sayings urge readers to abandon Jewish practices (see logia 6, 14, 27, 53 and 104), which suggests that the text represents some development in Christianity from Jesus' own time, particularly with its disapproval of circumcision (log. 53), a practice still in contention in the letters of Paul. Yet in one saying (log. 12) Jesus is asked, 'We know that you will leave us. Who will be great among us?' He responds, 'Wherever you have come, you will go to James the Righteous, for whose sake heaven and earth came to be.' James, the brother of Jesus, is usually associated with Jewish Christianity.

The gospel also gives a major role to Thomas who, alone of the apostles, is taken aside by Jesus and told special sayings. Peter, the apostle given primacy in the canonical Gospels, appears in the gospel's final saying (log. 114), where he says, 'Mary should leave us, for females are not worthy of the life.' Jesus responds, 'Look, I am going to guide her in order to make her male, so that she too may become a living spirit resembling you males. For every female who makes herself male will enter the kingdom of heaven.' It is a curious story. On the surface, it looks misogynistic, but likely the male–female qualities are to be read symbolically (Jesus cannot literally 'make her male') and may relate to the elimination of various distinctions described in saying 22:

> When you make the two one, and make the inside like the outside and the outside like the inside and the upper like the lower; and you make the male and the female be a single one, with the male no longer being male and the female no longer female . . . then you will enter the kingdom.

Scholarship on the origins of the *Gospel of Thomas* is divided between those who argue for early composition independent of the canonical Gospels and those who argue for late composition dependent upon the New Testament Gospels and other canonical texts. If the *Gospel of Thomas* is indeed a witness to Jesus' sayings in more raw form, then it will be a very important text for re-constructing Jesus' teachings and activities. Sometimes this has led to characterizations of Jesus as a proto-feminist and a wise man, not a supernatural Son of God. But the lack of miracles in the text and the absence of resurrection theology should not obscure the fact that *Thomas*'s Jesus is no mere human. He is still a mysterious, otherworldly figure who has come into the world and taken on flesh (log. 28), and who proclaims of himself, 'It is I who am the light upon them all. It is I who am the all. It is from me that the all has come, and to me that the all has extended' (log. 77).

The *Gospel of Philip*

In the same book from the Nag Hammadi Library that contains the *Gospel of Thomas* is found our only surviving copy of the *Gospel of Philip*. Scholars believe the gospel to be a product of the school of Valentinus, a second-century Egyptian Christian teacher who was later declared an arch-heretic. If so, the gospel must be dated to at least the late second century. There are indications in the text that it may have been composed in Syria.

The *Gospel of Philip* is not really an apocryphal Christian text at all. It reads instead like a sourcebook of Valentinian ideas relating to salvation, sacraments and ethics. These statements come in a variety of forms, including aphorisms, metaphors, parables, discourses and sayings, and, like the sayings in the *Gospel of Thomas*, are rather haphazardly organized. Of the 17 sayings attributed to Jesus in the text, eight of them are not found in the canonical Gospels; and it is these sayings that are of interest to scholars of the Christian Apocrypha.

Two particular statements in the text – one containing a saying – have captured readers' imaginations because they deal with the relationship between Jesus and Mary Magdalene. The first of these states, 'Three women always walked with the master: Mary his mother, [his] sister, and Mary of Magdala, who is called his companion. For "Mary" is the name of his sister, his mother, and his companion' (59.6–11). This notion of Mary as the 'companion' of Jesus is expanded a few statements later:

> The companion of the [Saviour] is Mary of Magdala. The [Saviour loved] her more than [all] the disciples, [and he] kissed her often on her [mouth]. The other [disciples] . . . said to him, 'Why do you love her more than all of us?' The Saviour answered and said to them, 'Why don't I love you like her?' (63.32—64.5)

Dan Brown's novel *The Da Vinci Code* made much of these statements to further its plotline that Jesus and Mary Magdalene were married and produced a child. The novel's antagonist, Grail scholar Leigh Teabing, explains that 'the word *companion*, in those days, literally meant *spouse*' (p. 246). True scholars, however, contend that the word used here for companion means 'friend' or 'associate', not 'spouse'. Readers should also be cautioned from seeing anything sexual about the exchange of kisses between Jesus and Mary. Early Christians regularly engaged in the ritual of the kiss of peace (see Romans 16.16; 1 Thessalonians 5.26) – today more often performed as a handshake. And *Philip* elsewhere associates this kiss explicitly with the exchange of knowledge from teacher to student: 'For it is by a kiss that the perfect [that is, those who have acquired knowledge] conceive and give birth. For this reason we also kiss one another' (59.2–4).

Clearly, *Philip*'s portrayals of Jesus and Mary should not be read too literally. At most these statements indicate that Mary was afforded respect by the author as someone intimate, but not necessarily sexually intimate, with Jesus. Perhaps the statements should be read even more symbolically. As with the *Gospel of Thomas*, *Philip* envisions salvation as a process of restoring primordial unity:

> If the female had not separated from the male, the female and the male would not have died. The separation of male and female was the beginning of death. Christ came to heal the separation that was from the beginning and reunite the two, in order to give life to those who died through separation and unite them. (70.9–17)

This union, of course, is not sexual, but spiritual, recombining the male and female aspects of humanity. Jesus and Mary may be seen as the model for this process, making the two one and thus ushering in the kingdom of God.

Sources and studies

The *Gospel of Thomas* can be found in Ehrman–Pleše, *The Apocryphal Gospels*, and the *Gospel of Philip* in Marvin Meyer, *The Nag Hammadi Scriptures*, pp. 157–86.

Letters of Jesus

It is traditionally believed that Jesus did not write anything himself; all we have are accounts of his life and teachings by his disciples and by disciples of disciples. The apocryphal Jesus, however, was a prolific letter writer. The earliest of these letters makes up part of the *Abgar Correspondence*. Abgar was the king of Edessa in eastern Syria from 4 BCE to 7 CE and from 13 to 50 CE. According to the *Correspondence*, an ailing Abgar, having heard of Jesus' healing abilities, writes to Jesus and asks him to journey to Edessa and heal him of his affliction. Jesus responds in his own letter with regrets, saying: 'I must accomplish everything I was sent here to do, and after accomplishing them ascend to the One who sent me.' But he promises Abgar relief: 'After I have ascended I will send you one of my disciples to heal your illness and to provide life both to you and to those who are with you.'

Some versions of the *Correspondence* include an additional gift to Abgar. Jesus writes, 'Your city will be blessed, and the enemy will no longer prevail over it.' These words lend a magical quality to the letter, a quality taken great advantage of by the people of Edessa. The pilgrim Egeria, who visited the city in 384 (see *Peregrinatio Egeriae* 17—19), reports that the people of Edessa carried the letter into battle and affixed a copy of it to the gates of the city. Christians throughout the ancient world, concerned about their personal protection, carried their own copies of the *Correspondence* in amulets; sometimes the letter was even inscribed on buildings to guard them from harm. The blessings promised by the letter guaranteed its popularity – versions are known in Greek, Latin, Syriac, Georgian, Ethiopian, Coptic, Armenian, Arabic, Persian and Slavonic, and parts of the story are found also incorporated in other texts, such as the Syriac *Life of the Blessed Virgin Mary*, and the Syriac and Armenian versions of the *Legend of the Thirty Pieces of Silver*.

But is it authentic? As exciting as it would be to have a letter written by Jesus, the *Correspondence* likely was composed in the third century, not the first. It seems to have played a role in conflicts between Christian groups in the East competing with one another for followers. Our earliest witness to the *Correspondence* is the historian Eusebius (263–339). He claims to have found the letters in the archives of Edessa and provides a translation of them from Syriac into Greek (*Ecclesiastical History* 1.13.5). He includes also a sequel to the letter in which the apostle Thomas sends the apostle Thaddaeus, one of the 70 disciples mentioned in Luke 10.1, to Abgar after Jesus' death. Thaddaeus heals Abgar and remains in Edessa to preach and heal others. An expanded account of the conversions and healings in Edessa is found in the Syriac *Doctrine of Addai*, though here the apostle is named Addai, not Thaddaeus. In this text, Abgar has Hannan, the keeper of the archives and the king's painter, carry his letter to Jesus and Jesus dictates to Hannan his reply. Hannan then returns to Edessa with his report and brings with him a portrait he painted of Jesus. The goal of the *Correspondence* and its sequels appears to be to provide an early origin for orthodox Christianity in the East, where, according to Walter Bauer (see Chapter 1), heretical Christian groups first flourished. Eusebius uses the *Correspondence* to place orthodoxy, represented by Thaddaeus, in Edessa immediately after Jesus' death. The *Doctrine of Addai* works similarly but specifically combats a form of Christianity called Manichaeism. The text replaces the prominent Manichaean missionary Addai with an orthodox Addai, and the portrait of Mani, important in Manichaean worship, with a portrait of Jesus.

Another letter, this one not written by Jesus but bearing on Jesus' earthly life, is attributed to a first-century Roman official named Publius Lentulus. The *Epistle of Lentulus* is a fairly late text, with the earliest manuscript dated to the fifteenth century, but it was widely copied. Likely it was composed in Latin, but Syriac, Persian and Armenian versions also exist. The bulk of the text is a praiseworthy description of Jesus, who, among other things, is said to have

> a brow smooth and very calm, with a face without a wrinkle or any blemish, which a moderate red colour makes beautiful; with the nose and mouth no fault at all can be found; having a full beard of the colour of his hair, not long, but a little forked at the chin.

The letter builds upon earlier descriptions of Jesus, such as the one found in works by the eighth century writer John of Damascus, and contributed to portrayals of Jesus in subsequent iconography. It became so popular that, even up to a century ago, it was considered by many to be a reliable description of Jesus.

Sources and studies

The *Abgar Correspondence* is found in Ehrman–Pleše, *The Apocryphal Gospels*. However, for the *Epistle of Lentulus* look in J. K. Elliott, *The Apocryphal New Testament*. The *Doctrine of Addai* has been translated into English by George Phillips.

The Christian Apocrypha are rich with traditions about the life of Jesus not included in the New Testament Gospels. We learn from them the names of his grandparents, details about the life of his mother, about his infancy in Egypt and his childhood in Nazareth. They give us remarkable new teachings, additional stories, letters, even a physical description of Jesus. But few scholars would argue that much of this material has historical value, at least not for revealing anything new about Jesus or his family. The texts do, however, tell us much about early Christianity. As mentioned in Chapter 1, Christians liked to 'think with stories', using early Christian figures as characters in narratives to express their own beliefs, anxieties and concerns as they negotiated an often hostile world. The texts were all written by and for Christians, but they reflect conflicts with outsiders, such as Graeco-Roman polytheists (or 'pagans') and Jews, and most of all, other Christians who had views different from their own.

Readers of the Christian Apocrypha are often surprised at the amount of variety of thought and practice in early Christianity; so much that it is difficult to determine what form of Christianity has the greatest claim for legitimacy and, by extension, which Jesus is the true Jesus. We will revisit this problem in Chapter 6 when we examine modern reactions to recent interest in the Christian Apocrypha. For now, simply enjoy the texts for the fascinating and entertaining stories they tell and for what they reveal, not so much about the life of Jesus, but about the lives of Christians.

4

Passion and resurrection gospels

In this chapter we turn from texts about the life and teachings of Jesus to texts that focus on the climax of the canonical Gospels: the Passion and resurrection of Jesus. It is widely believed among New Testament scholars that the Passion Narrative – the account of Jesus' arrest, trial, suffering and crucifixion – was one of the earliest pieces of Christian literature, influencing all of the Gospel writers when crafting their accounts of the events. As for the resurrection, all four of the canonical Gospels have different ways of demonstrating that Jesus had risen from the grave – from Mark's empty tomb, to Matthew's meeting of the apostles and Jesus in Galilee, Luke's tale of the two disciples on the road to Emmaus, John's fish-fry with the apostles, as well as others. Paul, too, lists a number of resurrection appearances (1 Corinthians 15.3–8).

We noted some aspects of scholarship on the Passion and resurrection of Jesus in Chapter 3 with our discussion of the *Gospel of Peter*, which contains a fifth account of these events. While there are few who agree that *Peter* is a better witness to this Passion Narrative than the canonical Gospels, *Peter*'s use of the material illustrates its importance for Christians, both in antiquity and up to today. Other writers from antiquity joined *Peter* in taking traditions about Jesus' death and resurrection and presenting them anew. Sometimes they keep much of what is found in the canonical Gospels, merely harmonizing the accounts and adding more detail, but at other times they completely reinterpret the events – perhaps as a direct challenge to proto-orthodox teachings – to reflect different understandings of Jesus' mission for humanity. To these writers, Jesus did not suffer and die on the cross after all, and there was no need for him to rise from the grave.

The *Revelation of Peter*

Among the texts of the Nag Hammadi Library is this short account of a conversation between Jesus and Peter set during the arrest and crucifixion of Jesus. The fourth-century Coptic manuscript from the collection is our only copy of the text, though it likely was composed in Greek some time in the third century. It opens with Peter sitting with Jesus in the Temple in Jerusalem. Jesus warns Peter that what he tells him will be difficult for some to accept:

> Now listen to the things I am telling you in secret and keep them. Do not tell them to the children of this age. For they will denounce you during these ages, since they are ignorant of you, but they will praise you when there is knowledge. (73.14–22)

Part of this difficult teaching is a vision, the 'revelation' of the text's title, in which Peter sees Jesus arrested and crucified. He asks,

> What do I see, Lord? Is it really you they are seizing, and are you holding on to me? And who is the one smiling and laughing above the cross? Is it someone else whose feet and hands they are hammering? (81.7–14)

Jesus answers,

> The one you see smiling and laughing above the cross is the living Jesus. The one into whose hands and feet they are driving nails is his fleshly part, the substitute for him. They are putting to shame the one who came into being in the likeness of the living Jesus. (81.15–23)

The text is making a distinction here between the body of the human Jesus of Nazareth and the living Jesus, the divine Christ, who temporarily inhabited it. The enemies of Christ have killed Jesus of Nazareth, but not the living Jesus, who laughs at their failure.

This idea that Jesus did not suffer the pain and humiliation of crucifixion (shared also by other texts, such as the *Acts of John* and the *Second Discourse of the Great Seth*, another text from the Nag Hammadi Library) is a challenge to proto-orthodox Christianity's position (explained in Chapter 1) that Jesus was crucified and rose from the grave in the flesh – what *Seth* calls 'the doctrine of a dead man' (60.22). In *Peter*, the author even calls the proto-orthodox view 'heresy' (74.22) and takes issue with the group's ecclesiastical hierarchy: 'there are others among those outside our number who call themselves bishops and deacons, as if they received authority from God, but they bow before the judgement of the leaders. These people are dry canals' (79.22–31). The proto-orthodox position eventually won the day, but these writings illustrate effectively that, in the early centuries, others held different views about the death and resurrection of Jesus, each considering itself 'orthodox'.

The *Gospel of Judas*

In 2006 the media were abuzz over a newly found text that its translators claimed would transform the traditional view of Judas, the infamous and often demonized betrayer of Jesus. This *Gospel of Judas*, they said, casts Judas as a hero, not a villain. The gospel seems to have originated in the middle of the second century. Irenaeus, writing around 180, mentions it as a product of a group known as the Cainites (*Against Heresies* 1.31.1). Today, only a single copy exists, the third-/fourth-century Coptic translation from the Codex Tchacos (see Chapter 2).

The story is set in Jesus' final week. It begins with, 'The secret revelatory discourse that Jesus spoke with Judas Iscariot in the course of a week, three days before his passion', and ends with Judas's betrayal. The text's theology is clearly Gnostic (see the description in Chapter 1). This is evident in the distinction made between the god of this world – named Saklas here but identified as the God of the Hebrew Scriptures – and a higher being dwelling in the highest heaven. Jesus is portrayed as an agent of this higher being. But perhaps more surprising to readers is that the apostles, despite being followers of Jesus, are portrayed as worshippers of Saklas. Jesus laughs at the apostles for performing the Eucharist meal, because their thanks go, not to the true God, but to the god of this world. Later they report to Jesus a vision of a temple with 12 priests at an altar receiving offerings. Of those who bring offerings, they say, [some abstain for] two weeks. [Some] sacrifice their own children, others their wives, while praising and blaming each other. Some have sex with men. Some perform acts of [murder]. Some commit all sorts of sins and lawless deeds. And the men who stand [before] the altar call upon your [name]. (38.14–26)

Jesus tells the apostles that they are the 12 priests in the vision, and the sacrifices are the people they lead astray.

Judas is not included in this group of 12; he stands outside their number and alone of the characters in the gospel understands who Jesus is. But does that make him a hero? Because of the damage suffered by the manuscript and the puzzling terminology used by the gospel's author, scholars are divided about the gospel's portrayal of Judas. As the 'thirteenth daimon' (44.21) is Judas literally demonic? Or is *daimon* to be understood as the more innocuous 'spirit', identifying Judas, therefore, as simply a divine being? Is Judas 'set apart' (46.16–18) for the generation of the saved? Or is he 'separated from' them? In one passage, Jesus tells Judas, 'those [who] bring sacrifices to Sakla . . . God . . . everything evil. But you will exceed all of them. For you will sacrifice the man who bears me' (56.11–21). Does this mean that Judas is praiseworthy for being *better* than the apostles, particularly for fulfilling his role as betrayer? Or does he 'exceed' them by being *worse* because his crime was the sacrifice of Jesus?

A few more fragments of the Tchacos manuscript have recently come into the hands of scholars; these may help to settle the debate over Judas's role in the text. Wherever that discussion goes, what remains interesting about the gospel are the features it shares with the *Revelation of Peter* and the other texts mentioned above: the laughing Jesus, the separation between the divine Christ and the human Jesus, and the criticism of proto-orthodox Christianity. Even as early as the middle of the second century, voices were raised against teachings about the Passion of Jesus that are now considered essential to the Christian faith.

The *Book of the Cock*

Judas appears again in a peculiar text that stars a talking rooster. The *Book of the Cock*, though believed to have been composed in Greek in or around Jerusalem in the fifth or sixth century, is now available only in Ethiopic. In Ethiopia, the *Book of the Cock* attained a semi-canonical status, with parts of the text incorporated into the Holy Week Lectionary reporting the Acts of the Passion.

The text recounts the final three days of Jesus' life. It begins with Jesus and the disciples on the Mount of Olives. There a talking rock announces the imminent betrayal of Judas. Then the group adjourns to the house of Simon the Pharisee to celebrate Passover. Simon's wife Akrosennā prepares a rooster for their meal. But Jesus brings the rooster to life and gives it the ability to speak so that it will spy on Judas. The rooster follows Judas home and watches as Judas sleeps with his wife – a notable event, as the text states that true followers of Jesus no longer 'commit this kind of sin' (4.9). Like Herod Antipas's wife, whom the Gospels portray as the evil force behind the death of John the Baptist, Judas's wife plays a large role in Judas's villainy. She says to him:

> I am going to counsel you; listen to me. Go to the Jews and receive your reward from them; take them to the place where Jesus is, hand him over to them so that they may do what they want, and come home quickly.   (4.10)

Judas then works with Paul, arranging between them a signal so that Paul can arrest Jesus. The rooster then flies back to Jesus with his report. As a reward Jesus sends him to heaven for a thousand years.

The text continues with a harmonization of the Passion Narratives from the canonical Gospels, though with a few alarming differences. Not only does Paul follow through with the arrest of Jesus but he even places the crown of thorns on Jesus' head. Paul's role here contradicts the canonical book of Acts, which makes it clear that Paul did not know the earthly Jesus; he was introduced to the risen Jesus through a vision. Acts also reveals that Paul was a persecutor of Christians before he became one of the movement's most important leaders. The *Book of the Cock* has projected Paul's villainy earlier in Christian history. Such negative portrayals of Paul are often found in Jewish-Christian texts (see the discussion of the *Pseudo-Clementine Romance* in Chapter 5);

perhaps the traditions incorporated into the *Book of the Cock* also have Jewish-Christian origins.

Sources and studies

The *Revelation of Peter* and the *Gospel of Judas* are available in Marvin Meyer, *The Nag Hammadi Scriptures*, pp. 487–97 and 755–69. Meyer is a proponent of the view that Judas is portrayed heroically in the text; for the contrary position, that Judas remains a villain, see April DeConick, *The Thirteenth Apostle*. For a summary and study of the *Book of the Cock*, see Pierluigi Piovanelli, 'Exploring the Ethiopic *Book of the Cock*'.

The Pilate Cycle

If you're uncomfortable with the arch-villain Judas portrayed as a hero, wait till you see what the Pilate Cycle of texts does with Pilate, the Prefect of Judaea, who was chiefly responsible for the death of Jesus. Despite his culpability, the canonical Gospels tend to minimize Pilate's role in the crucifixion. He is portrayed as reluctant to execute Jesus, and only does so when coerced by the Jewish leadership (John 19.12) or urged forward by a mob who, when offered the opportunity to free Jesus, call instead for the release of the 'bandit' Barabbas (Mark 15.6–14 and parallels; John 18.39–40). Likely, this presentation of the events is precipitated by the need for early Christians to present themselves, through tales of Jesus, as a group that is not a threat to Roman sovereignty – Jesus was executed because of conflict with his fellow Jews, not because Pilate considered him a menace. The texts in the Pilate Cycle continue this tendency, heaping further scorn on the Jews and going so far at times as elevating Pilate to the status of a saint.

The anchor text in the Pilate Cycle is the *Public Records about Our Lord Jesus Christ, Composed under Pontius Pilate*, better known as the *Acts of Pilate*. Several early writers mention official reports of Pilate about Jesus (Justin Martyr, *First Apology* 35.9; 48.3; Tertullian, *Apology* 21.24; Eusebius, *Ecclesiastical History* 1.9.3–4; 9.5.1; 9.7.1; and Epiphanius, *Refutation of all Heresies* 50.1). Scholars usually dismiss these reports as fictions, though the *Acts* may have been written to give fact to the reports. The text likely was composed in the fourth or fifth century. The Greek A version is considered to be the best representative of the tradition; this was translated into Latin, Syriac, Palestinian Aramaic, Coptic, Georgian, Armenian and several old European vernaculars. The Latin tradition, renamed the *Gospel of Nicodemus* in the twelfth century, features a number of transformations and expansions, including the addition of Jesus' *Descent into Hell* (discussed further below). The *Acts of Pilate* is perhaps the most widespread and popular apocryphal Christian text – it is found in more than 500 manuscripts, contributed to medieval passion plays such as the fifteenth-century N-Town Plays (mentioned in Chapter 2), and reflects (perhaps even helped create) key points of Christian teaching about the death and resurrection of Jesus.

The *Acts of Pilate* begins with a prologue crediting Nicodemus (featured prominently in the Gospel of John, see 3.1–10; 7.50–52; 19.39–42) with writing down the 'public records' of the trial before Pilate. The first nine chapters harmonize and expand upon the canonical Gospels' accounts of the trial. But the roles of the Jewish leaders, led by the high priests Annas and Caiaphas, are amplified. They stubbornly refuse to accept Jesus' divine origins, continually urging Pilate to crucify Jesus and later working to cover up evidence of the resurrection. The Romans, on the other hand, treat him like a king; even the images on the standards of the Roman soldiers bow to him. Pilate tries valiantly to prevent the execution of Jesus but, as in the canonical Gospels, he eventually relents, telling the Jews to 'see to it [them]selves' (9.4). Pilate's wife, who Matthew (27.19) says was troubled by a dream of Jesus, is here named Procla and is described as a convert to Judaism (2.1). As the trial progresses, several characters from the canonical Gospels come forward in Jesus' defence, including several people who were healed by Jesus, such as the woman suffering from haemorrhages (Mark 5.25–34 and parallels), here given the name Berenice (meaning 'bearer of victory'; Veronica in Latin). Names are given also to the two thieves crucified with Jesus: Dysmas and Gestas.

After a quick recounting of the crucifixion (chs 10—11), the text turns its focus to Joseph of Arimathea, the 'respected member of the council' (Mark 15.43) who was granted the body of Jesus. In the *Acts of Pilate*, Joseph is imprisoned by the Jews as a Christian sympathizer. But somehow Joseph escapes. Reports then come in, from the guards at the tomb and from Galilean rabbis, that Jesus has risen from the grave. The leaders begin to worry. They search for Jesus but, instead, find Joseph at his home in Arimathea. Joseph tells them that Jesus appeared to him in prison and brought him to Arimathea. After the leaders interrogate Joseph and the Galilean rabbis, they conclude, 'If [Jesus'] remembrance extends until the year which is called Jubilee, know that he will prevail forever and will raise a new people for himself' (16.7). The *Acts of Pilate* ends, then, on a conciliatory note, with the Jews – both the leaders and the people – open to the possibility that Jesus is the Messiah after all.

Joseph's imprisonment and escape are retold in another text from the Pilate Cycle: the *Narrative of Joseph of Arimathea*. The *Narrative*, told as a first-person account by Joseph, was composed in Greek sometime after the *Acts of Pilate*, perhaps as late as the sixth century. The focus of the text is the two criminals. 'The first, named Gestas,' Joseph says, 'used to murder travelers with the sword and he stripped others naked; he hung women head downwards from their ankles and cut off their breasts; he drank blood from the limbs of infants' (2). The second, Demas (a slight variation of 'Dysmas' from the *Acts of Pilate*), is a Galilean, and is described as a Robin Hood figure, robbing the rich but helping the poor. He is imprisoned for stealing a book of the law from the Temple. Judas is then introduced as the son-in-law of Caiaphas and a false follower of Jesus, hired to spy on the group by 'all the multitude of the Jews' (3). Through Judas's schemes, Jesus is arrested for Demas's crime. After his arrest and trial, Jesus is crucified with the robbers and makes his promise to Demas: 'today you will be with me in Paradise' (Luke 23.43). Jesus even dictates a letter (while on the cross!) for Demas to use as his passport into heaven. The *Narrative* then recounts Joseph's imprisonment from the *Acts of Pilate*. But this time, when Jesus appears to Joseph in his cell, Demas is there too, still holding his cross. The thief has a letter for Jesus from the cherubim and the six-winged creatures (see Revelation 4.8), acknowledging his acceptance into paradise. After three days spent with Joseph in

Galilee, Jesus and Demas disappear and Joseph is magically whisked to his home in Arimathea.

The other texts in the Pilate Cycle continue the story of Pilate after the trial, presenting his death as either the glorious martyrdom of a saint or the just desserts of a murderous villain. As early as the late second century, Christians claimed Pilate as one of their own. Tertullian (*c.* 160–225 CE) writes that the Roman prefect 'was already a Christian with respect to his inner conviction' (*Apology* 21.24). Eventually, the Coptic and Ethiopian churches declared him a saint. In the *Letter of Pilate to Claudius* and the *Report of Pontius Pilate* Pilate is forgiven for his role in Jesus' death, by either a voice from heaven or Jesus himself. Other Church writers are less sympathetic to Pilate. Eusebius (*Ecclesiastical History* 2.7) says that Pilate committed suicide – 'divine justice, it seems, was not slow to overtake him'. The same perspective is reflected in a number of Pilate Cycle texts – the *Letter of Tiberius to Pilate*, the *Vengeance of the Saviour*, the *Cure of Tiberius* and the *Death of Pilate* – in which Pilate dies unceremoniously at either his own hand or that of the emperor. In the *Vengeance of the Saviour*, Pilate's final resting place is revealed to be Switzerland's Lake Lucerne, 'where even now,' the text says, 'according to some reports, certain diabolical contrivances are said to boil up'. Another tradition has it that Pilate's body rests in the Lago di Pilato (Lake of Pilate) in Italy.

The later Pilate Cycle texts take delight also in describing the calamities that befell the Jews as a result of Jesus' death. In the *Report of Pontius Pilate*, the Jews, not Pilate or his fellow Romans, received divine retribution for their actions; in the earthquakes that attended Jesus' death, 'many of the Jews died, being engulfed and swallowed in the chasms in that night, so that their bodies could no longer be found' (10). In other texts (such as the *Handing over of Pilate*, the *Letter of Tiberius to Pilate* and the *Vengeance of the Saviour*), the emperor, incensed by the Jews for killing a clearly righteous man, sends troops to lay waste to the nation – an anachronistic account of the Jewish War, which took place 30 years later in the reign of the emperor Nero and was carried out, at first, by his general Vespasian and later by the emperor Titus. The only character who seems to benefit from the Pilate Cycle's expansions of the Passion Narrative is Veronica, the woman suffering from haemorrhages who was given name in the *Acts of Pilate*. In the *Cure of Tiberius* and the *Death of Pilate*, we learn that Veronica carried an image of Jesus' face on a cloth. The tradition may have grown out of a false etymology of Veronica's name as meaning 'true icon' (*vera eikon*). By the fifteenth century, Veronica and her image of Christ became part of the Stations of the Cross, a series of artistic representations still found in Catholic churches of Jesus on the way to his crucifixion. At the sixth station, Veronica wipes Jesus' face, receiving his image on her cloth.

The Pilate Cycle is a rich contributor to Christian traditions about the Passion of Jesus. Various anonymous characters from the canonical Gospels receive names and other details about their lives, the final fates of Pilate and his wife are revealed (in several ways), and certain stories are remembered in iconography or associated with auspicious landmarks. Sadly, the texts also develop further the notion that the Jews, not Pilate, are to be held chiefly responsible for Jesus' crucifixion. A few go so far as to portray the siege of Jerusalem as divine 'vengeance' on Jews for the death of Jesus. As exciting as it is to recognize so many mainstream Christian traditions within the Pilate Cycle, it is unfortunate that it also contains such virulent anti-Semitism, and that the Cycle has contributed to the mistreatment of Jews by Christians over the centuries.

Sources and studies

Most of the Pilate Cycle texts discussed here can be found in Ehrman–Pleše, *The Apocryphal Gospels*.

The *Descent into Hell*

Jesus was sent to earth to bring salvation to humanity. But what about the righteous who perished before the arrival of Jesus? The matriarchs and patriarchs of the Hebrew Scriptures – Abraham, Sarah, Moses, David, Esther – are they not also worthy of salvation? According to Christian teaching, at his death, Jesus descended to hell to preach to the dead, and those who responded to his teachings followed him into paradise. The doctrine of the Harrowing of Hell, as it is called, has some biblical support – according to 1 Peter, Jesus, after his death, 'went and made a proclamation to the spirits in prison' (3.19) and later the letter states, 'the gospel was proclaimed even to the dead' (4.6). Early Church writers, such as Justin Martyr and Augustine, echoed and expanded upon 1 Peter's remarks. But the most elaborate treatment of the doctrine is found in the *Descent into Hell* (or the *Descensus ad Inferos*), a section of the Latin versions of the *Acts of Pilate* (called the *Gospel of Nicodemus*, but also found in the Greek B version of the *Acts of Pilate*).

The text begins with Joseph of Arimathea reporting to Annas and Caiaphas, the high priests at Jesus' trial, about the dead saints who have been seen roaming around Jerusalem (see Matthew 27.52–54). Two of these saints, Karinus and Leucius, identified as the sons of Simeon (the 'righteous and devout' man who blesses the infant Jesus in Luke 2.25–35), are interrogated by the Jewish leaders. The remainder of the text is an account of everything they saw and heard. We learn that Satan and Hades – the Greek god of the underworld, presented here both as a speaking character and as the underworld itself – conspired to have Jesus killed and now Satan needs to keep Jesus within Hades. Jesus arrives in Hades in might and glory:

> the bronze gates were crushed and the iron bars were smashed, and all the dead who were bound were released from their bonds, and we along with them. And the King of glory came in, as a human; and all the dark places of Hades were enlightened.
>
> (21.3)

Satan, not Jesus, is left bound in Hades where he will remain until Jesus' second coming. All the patriarchs, prophets, martyrs and ancestors are then led away to paradise. Once there, they meet Enoch and Elijah, who rose up to heaven body and soul (Genesis 5.24; 2 Kings 2.11; Hebrews 11.5), and the good thief who was sent to paradise by Jesus. Here Karinus and Leucius finish their account and disappear, headed off to their own heavenly reward. The *Descent into Hell* vividly answers questions occasioned by 1 Peter's vague remarks about Jesus preaching to the dead. The text enjoyed great popularity, not only because of its incorporation into the widely copied *Gospel of Nicodemus,* but also because elements of the text were included in several medieval homilies.

Jesus' time in hell is featured also in two texts attributed to Bartholomew, an apostle held in esteem in the Coptic Church. The first of these, the *Questions of Bartholomew,* features a dialogue between the apostle and the resurrected Jesus. It is available in Greek, Latin and Old Slavonic, and has been dated, rather imprecisely, to some time between the second and fifth centuries. Other prominent followers of Jesus appear in the text – including his mother Mary, Peter, John and Mary Magdalene – but they all seem too shy or too frightened to approach Jesus. Bartholomew is the only one who dares to ask him questions. He begins, saying,

> I looked and I saw that you vanished away from the cross, and I heard only a voice in the parts under the earth, and great wailing and gnashing of teeth all of a sudden. Tell me, Lord, where did you go to from the cross? (1.6)

Jesus reveals that he descended to hell, bound him in chains, brought up the patriarchs and then returned to the cross. We learn also that few of those who have died will ascend to paradise. Jesus says that 30,000 souls depart from hell every day, but only 53 are found righteous, and only three of these are allowed to enter paradise (1.33).

The second Bartholomew text has no title, but scholars have long referred to it as the *Book of the Resurrection of Jesus Christ by Bartholomew the Apostle.* The lengthy book was composed in Coptic around the fifth or sixth century. Three incomplete manuscripts exist, along with several fragments, one of which contains a parallel to the *Book of the Cock,* but many scholars now think some of these fragments belong to other texts. In the story, Jesus is visited in his tomb by Death. He awakes, mounts a chariot of cherubim, descends to hell, binds the demons and releases the souls of the holy. Only three of the dead remain in hell: Herod, Cain and Judas. His work in hell complete, Jesus comes back to earth and reveals himself to the women at the tomb. Then Jesus ascends to heaven with all the holy souls.

Sources and studies

The *Descent into Hell* is available in Ehrman–Pleše's translation of *Acts of Pilate* Greek B. The Bartholomew texts are in J. K. Elliott's *The Apocryphal New Testament*, pp. 652–72, though Elliott gives only a summary of the *Book of the Resurrection*; for the full text see E. A. Wallis Budge, *Coptic Apocrypha in the Dialect of Upper Egypt*, pp. 1–48 and 179–230. To learn more about the Harrowing of Hell doctrine, particularly its use in medieval harmonies, see John A. McCulloch, *The Harrowing of Hell*.

Post-resurrection appearances and teachings

The story of Jesus does not end with his death. Indeed, integral to Christian belief is that Jesus conquered death. But not all Christians agree on the details of Jesus' triumph. According to the canonical Gospels, Jesus returned in the flesh. Then, in Acts, he remains with the apostles after his resurrection for 40 days, teaching them about the kingdom of God (Acts 1.3). Some apocryphal texts expand upon this tradition, using these 40 days to have Jesus communicate additional teachings. In other texts, Jesus routinely appears in ghostly form, delivering new teachings, directing his disciples in their missionary efforts, or guiding visionaries on ghastly tours of the underworld. These texts are too often neglected in studies of the Christian Apocrypha because they do not focus on Jesus' earthly life; but they contain some fascinating teachings and fantastic visions, some of which have had a profound impact on Christian tradition.

The *Apocryphon* (or *Secret Book*) *of John*

The *Apocryphon of John*, a classic of Christian Gnostic thought, consists almost entirely of a Creation story told by the risen Jesus to the apostle John. We have four copies of this text: three in the Nag Hammadi Library, and a fourth in the Berlin Codex (discussed in Chapter 2). All four are independent translations from Greek. The text also appears in summary in Irenaeus's *Against Heresies* (1.29–30). Likely, it was written around the middle of the second century.

87

Secret John opens with John, the son of Zebedee, en route to the Temple. A Pharisee asks him about Jesus and says, 'This Nazarene really has deceived you, filled your ears with lies, closed [your minds], and turned you from the traditions of your ancestors' (1.12–17). Distressed about this, John withdraws to the wilderness and asks himself a series of questions: 'How was the Saviour chosen? Why was he sent into the world by his Father? Who is his Father who sent him? To what kind of eternal realm shall we go?' (1.21–29). In response, the heavens open and Jesus appears, bathed in light. He then answers John's questions with a Creation myth (also called a cosmogony), pausing now and then to address additional queries from John. This kind of questioning is typical of the post-resurrection texts, where the risen Jesus and the disciples enter into a teacher–student dialogue regarding secret teachings about Jesus' true origins, the way to salvation, and the fate of humanity.

As mentioned back in Chapter 1, the cosmogonies are a blend of Greek thought and Judaeo-Christian Creation myths. *Secret John* offers one of the most elaborate of the cosmogonies. It's a real challenge to read. Apparently, discovering one's origins and the route to salvation was not meant to be easy. One of the more shocking sections of the text retells the story of Adam and Eve's expulsion from the Garden of Eden. After the two eat from the tree of knowledge, Yaldabaoth (the evil version of the Old Testament God) casts them out of Eden and, forced to drink the water of forgetfulness, they lose knowledge of their origins once again. Then Yaldabaoth defiles Eve and thereby produces two sons: Cain and Abel, also named Elohim and Yahweh, the two names for God in the Hebrew Scriptures. According to *Secret John*, then, the evil Yaldabaoth introduces sex into the world and in a horrific manner – not surprising in a text written for a branch of Christianity that champions sexual abstinence. Also not surprising is that women are portrayed as a distraction from celibacy. 'To this day,' Jesus says in the text, 'sexual intercourse has persisted because of the first ruler. He planted sexual desire within the woman who belongs to Adam' (24.26–29). It's unfortunate to find this here, because the text otherwise features positive feminine imagery, particularly in the prominence given to Wisdom (Sophia) and the role of Barbelo as the Mother figure in the heavens and the guardian of humanity.

The lengthy cosmogony and salvation history finished, *Secret John* comes to a close with the ascension of Jesus. Before he leaves, Jesus says to John, 'I have told you everything for you to record and communicate secretly to your spiritual friends' (31.28–30). Now that secret knowledge is available to all who read this text.

The *Gospel of Mary*

Where *Secret John* has the apostle John communicate secret teaching, the *Gospel of Mary* gives that role to a woman: Mary Magdalene, known in Christian tradition as a repentant prostitute. The text is found in a fifth-century Coptic codex and in two fragmentary third-century Greek manuscripts from the Oxyrhynchus Papyri. Unfortunately, even the Coptic manuscript is incomplete; it is missing the first six pages and another four pages in the middle – roughly half the gospel.

The Coptic manuscript begins partway through a dialogue with the risen Jesus. Only two of the questions are preserved, one of which is asked by Peter. When Jesus departs, the disciples are distressed, worried that they will suffer as Jesus did. Mary comforts the men, leading Peter to ask her, 'Sister, we know that the Saviour loved you more than the other women. Tell us the words of the Saviour that you remember, which you know and we do not, since we did not hear them' (10.1–6). Mary tells of once speaking to Jesus after seeing him in a vision. After a large gap, the text resumes in the middle of Jesus' description of the ascent of the soul as it moves up past the powers of darkness that seek to keep it from reaching its final destination. Some of the disciples find Mary's story disturbing. Andrew says, 'these teachings are strange thoughts indeed' (17.14–15). And Peter, though earlier deferential to Mary, asks, 'Did he really speak with a woman secretly from us, not openly?' (17.18–20). Only Levi comes to Mary's defence, saying, 'Peter, you are always angry . . . If the Saviour made her worthy, who are you then, for your part, to cast her aside? Surely the Saviour knows her full well. That is why he loved her more than us' (18.6–16). The argument settled, the disciples go out into the world to teach and proclaim the gospel.

The *Gospel of Mary* is not the only text to feature a conflict between Mary and Peter. Recall the conclusion of the *Gospel of*

Thomas, where Peter says, 'Mary should leave us, for females are not worthy of the life' (114). The two square off also in the *Pistis Sophia*, a sprawling post-resurrection dialogue preserved in a fourth-century Coptic manuscript. A number of disciples take part in this dialogue – Mary the mother of Jesus, Philip, Peter, Martha, John, Andrew, Thomas, Matthew, James and Salome – but the majority of the questions (39 out of 46) are posed by Mary Magdalene. Peter is not happy with all the attention given to Mary. He says, 'My Lord, we are not able to suffer this woman who takes the opportunity from us, and does not allow anyone of us to speak, but she speaks many times' (36). And later, Mary worries about Peter's reaction if she speaks too much:

> My Lord, my mind is understanding at all times that I should come forward at any time and give the interpretation of the words which she spoke, but I am afraid of Peter, for he threatens me and he hates our race. (72)

Why are Peter and Mary portrayed this way in these texts? Early Christian groups often adopted particular disciples as representative of their community and its theology. Scholars speculate that the conflict between Mary and Peter represents a conflict between two branches of Christianity: one identifying with Peter and representing patriarchal proto-orthodoxy, and the other identifying with Mary and representing a more egalitarian Gnostic or mystical group. This idea is a tantalizing possibility, and the notion of an early proto-feminist form of Christianity is certainly attractive to modern Christians open to women holding leadership positions in their churches.

Scholarship on the *Gospel of Mary* has done much recently to dispel the notion that Mary Magdalene was a prostitute, a belief based on the erroneous association of Mary Magdalene with the woman with the alabaster jar in Luke 7.36–50. The woman in Luke is described as a sinner, and the traditional interpretation of the story characterizes the sin as prostitution. By at least the sixth century, the prostitute becomes merged with Mary Magdalene, who is described in the very next story as one of several women who provided financial support to Jesus (Luke 8.2–3). The *Gospel of Mary*'s treatment of Mary Magdalene is far truer to Luke's portrayal. The gospel has been used also by those, like novelist Dan

Brown, who seek to prove a romantic connection between Jesus and Mary. Peter's words to Mary, that 'the Saviour loved [her] more than the other women' (10.1–3), combined with similar statements in the *Gospel of Philip* (discussed in Chapter 3), certainly make Mary look important to Jesus, though none of this is evidence that the two were married.

Other post-resurrection appearances

Many of the post-resurrection texts are set in the form of dialogues in which the risen Jesus is posed questions by his apostles and other disciples, and Jesus answers them with new, often puzzling teachings. One of the earliest dialogue texts is the *Gospel of the Egyptians*, a second-century text preserved, like the Jewish-Christian gospels, only in quotations from early Church writers. It is mentioned disparagingly by Origen, Hippolytus and Epiphanius, but not so by Clement of Alexandria, who quotes the text six times in an attempt to correct a misreading of it by radical ascetics (named here 'Encratites'). All six quotations feature Salome, one of the women at the crucifixion and the tomb in Mark 15.40 and 16.1, and who also appears in the *Gospel of Thomas* 61, *Secret Mark*, and other texts. Salome asks Jesus several questions relating to celibacy. In one of the quotations Salome asks, 'How long will death prevail?' And Jesus answers, 'For as long as you women bear children.' The reply echoes the doctrine about re-establishing primeval unity we have encountered already in the gospels of *Thomas* and *Philip*. This connection is further established in a second quotation that is paralleled in the *Gospel of Thomas* 22 and 37 (as well as *2 Clement* 12.1–2):

> When Salome inquired when the things she had asked about would become known, the Lord replied: 'When you (pl.) trample on the garment of shame and when the two become one and the male with the female is neither male nor female.'
>
> (*Miscellanies* 3.92.2—93.1)

Clement of Alexandria writes in support of the text, arguing that the Encratites are reading it too literally, that, read properly, it does not disparage sex and procreation; but this is precisely what it appears to do. There is no way to know what the full text of the *Gospel of the Egyptians* was like – it's not even clear that its dialogue takes place after the resurrection – but if the exchanges with Salome are typical, its form and content make it fit well with other dialogue texts.

Five other dialogue texts appear in the Nag Hammadi Library: the *Book of Thomas the Contender*, the *Secret Book* (or *Apocryphon*) of *James*, the *Dialogue of the Saviour*, the *Letter of Peter to Philip* (also found in Codex Tchacos), and two texts each going by the name of the *Revelation of James*. As in *Secret John*, the questions asked by the apostles typically bear on the origins of humanity and the way to salvation. Several themes from the texts we looked at earlier resurface, including the negative portrayal of Peter – in the *Secret Book of James*, Peter, perhaps once again representing misguided proto-orthodox Christianity, struggles with Jesus' new teachings (see 13.26–36) – and Docetic understandings of the crucifixion (discussed in Chapter 1) – in the first *Revelation of James*, Jesus makes a distinction between the divine Christ and his human vessel: 'I am the one who was within me. Never did I suffer at all, and I was not distressed. These people did not harm me' (31.17–22). Asceticism, once again, is held up as the ideal state of being. In the *Book of Thomas*, for example, Jesus utters several woes, one against those who 'love intercourse and filthy association with the female' (144.8–10). To become perfect, Jesus says, one must 'lay down [one's] animal nature' (139.28) and be a contender ('one who struggles' against the passions) like Thomas. A similar viewpoint is expressed by Matthew in the *Dialogue of the Saviour*. Interpreting Jesus' command to 'pray in the place where there is no woman', Matthew says this means 'destroy the works of the female, not because there is another form of birth but because they should stop [giving birth]' (144.17–21).

The post-resurrection dialogue genre clearly was popular among Gnostic Christians, but it was also used by proto-orthodox Christians. The author of the anti-Gnostic *Epistle to the Apostles* (or *Epistula Apostolorum*) may have decided to use the same genre precisely because it was so valued by his adversaries. The *Epistle* was composed in Greek in the last quarter of the second century, but survives today only in Coptic, Ethiopic and a small Latin fragment. The goal of the text is revealed at the beginning of the Ethiopic text, which claims to have been written so that no one should follow the false apostles Simon and Cerinthus. The Simon mentioned here is the arch-heretic Simon Magus introduced in the canonical book of Acts (8.9–24); Cerinthus was a teacher from Asia Minor (Turkey) in the first half of the second century who subscribed to a Docetic view of Jesus (see the description in Irenaeus, *Against Heresies* 1.26.1). After this introduction, the text presents an overview of the life of Jesus featuring tales drawn from the canonical Gospels together with the story of Jesus and the teacher from the *Infancy Gospel of Thomas* (2—6) and a fully orthodox account of the crucifixion and resurrection (7—11).

Finally, we come to the meat of the text: Jesus remains with the apostles after his resurrection and passes on new teachings, sometimes occasioned by questions from the apostles, about his Incarnation, the coming persecution, the form Jesus will take when he returns, and when that will occur. The teachings place emphasis on resurrection in the flesh, both for Jesus and his faithful followers. Any who 'have taught another teaching' (29), like Simon and Cerinthus, will receive eternal punishment. Jesus also tells the Eleven that they will be joined soon by Paul (31—33), and provides details of his activities drawn from the book of Acts. The *Epistle* then concludes with Jesus ascending into heaven.

The *Epistle* affirms several key aspects of proto-orthodox thought. The virgin birth, Jesus' resurrection in the flesh, his Ascension and the second coming are all championed over the rival Docetic interpretation of Jesus promoted by Gnostic Christians. The apostles, too, are portrayed in a way that is conducive to proto-orthodoxy: as a cohesive group with Paul in its ranks and adhering to proto-orthodox views of Jesus. This portrayal differs much from the individual depictions of the apostles, with their heretical teachings and practices, that we will see in Chapter 5 with our look at apocryphal acts. Yet, surprisingly, there are some aspects of the text proto-orthodox Christians would have found objection-able – such as the childhood tale of Jesus as part of the summary of Jesus' life, and the Incarnation described as Jesus descending from heaven to earth in the form of an angel; these may have contributed to the *Epistle*'s censure. The *Epistle* illustrates well the notion that orthodox Christianity grew out of early proto-orthodox communities which held beliefs that were either retained, developed or abandoned in later centuries.

Sources and studies

The *Gospel of the Egyptians*, the *Gospel of Mary* and the *Gospel of Judas* can be read in Ehrman–Pleše, *The Apocryphal Gospels*, though the version of *Judas* used here is from Marvin Meyer's *The Nag Hammadi Scriptures*, the source also for the other Nag Hammadi dialogue texts. The full text of the *Pistis Sophia* is available in the critical edition by Carl Schmidt, and the *Epistle of the Apostles* is included in J. K. Elliott, *The Apocryphal New Testament*, pp. 555–88.

Apocalypses

In Christian texts, Jesus continues to appear to his apostles and other disciples even after the fateful 40 days of post-resurrection teachings. Such appearances are rare in canonical texts, but they do occur; the best known of these is Paul's encounter with Jesus on the road to Damascus in Acts (9.1–9). This is followed by two other appearances, to the disciple Ananias (9.10–17) and, in voice only, to Peter (10.13–15). Jesus similarly directs events in the apocryphal acts (a category of texts we will examine in the next chapter), as well as another group of texts called 'apocalypses'.

In apocalypses various biblical figures, both Old Testament and New, are taken on journeys to the heavens and granted visions of a time in the future when the community of the text's author will encounter terrible persecution. But those who suffer are promised an eternity spent in paradise, whereas the wicked, including the authors' enemies and those from within the communities who renounce the faith, will face punishment without end in hell. Apocalypses, both Jewish and Christian, come in two basic forms: those that feature a messianic figure who shows the visionary signs of the end time and the beginning of God's reign on earth, and those in which the visionary is taken on a tour of the heavens; there he, or she, sees where the righteous and the wicked will dwell when the end comes. Some apocalypses combine both forms.

The apocalypses of John

The earliest Christian apocalypse is the canonical book of Revelation ascribed to a certain John – often given the title John of Patmos, or John the Divine, to distinguish him from the apostle John. The focus of this text is the end-time battle between cosmic powers of good and evil, with Jesus leading the heavenly host against the forces of Satan and his agent on earth, the Beast. After Jesus' victory, Satan and his minions are thrown into a lake of fire, and the faithful are raised from death to live forever in a new heaven and a new earth ruled directly by God.

But the story does not end there for John; he is called on again to receive new visions in several apocryphal apocalypses. The most noteworthy of these is the *Apocalypse of Saint John the Theologian* (commonly known as *2 Apocalypse of John*), available in Greek and Arabic and perhaps composed in Syria in the fourth century. Written as a supplement to the canonical book of Revelation, the second apocalypse has John ask Jesus to give him additional details about his vision, such as a more detailed physical description of the Beast and more information about the conditions of life after the second coming. The righteous dead, whether children or senior citizens, will 'rise as thirty-year-olds' (10), Jesus says, and physical divisions will be no more:

> Just as the bees do not differ one from another, but are all of the same appearance and size, so every human-being will be at the resurrection. Not fair-skinned, nor red-skin, nor black, not Ethiopian nor different facial features, but all will rise with the same appearance and size. (11)

Additional Johannine apocalypses also exist, including the eighth-/ninth-century *Question and Answer to Saint John the Theologian from James the Lord's Brother* (or *3 Apocalypse of John*), an eleventh-century Coptic text called the *Mysteries of Saint John the Apostle and Holy Virgin* and a still-unpublished *4 Apocalypse of John* in Greek.

The *Apocalypse of Peter*

The *Apocalypse of Peter* is by far the most influential of the apocryphal apocalypses. It was so well regarded in antiquity that

Peter came very close to being included in the New Testament canon. Clement of Alexandria considered it Scripture, and it is listed alongside Revelation in the second-century list of books known as the Muratorian Canon (see the discussion in Chapter 1), though some Christians, the author says, do not want *Peter* to be read in church. Another canon list, from a sixth-century manuscript of the Pauline letters known as the Codex Claromontanus, includes as canonical both the *Apocalypse of Peter* and the *Acts of Paul*. Over time, the text fell out of use. Today it is preserved in several citations by early writers like Clement, along with a small third-/fourth-century Greek fragment from Egypt, the lengthier Greek fragment from Akhmim (with roughly half of the text), and a complete text from two Ethiopic manuscripts (dated to the fourteenth/fifteenth and eighteenth centuries).

The story is set just prior to the Transfiguration scene reported in the Synoptic Gospels (Mark 9.2–8 and parallels), where Jesus speaks to the apostles on the Mount of Olives. They say to him, 'Declare to us what are the signs of your coming and of the end of the world, that we may perceive and mark the time of your coming and instruct those who come after us' (1). One of these signs is the coming of a false messiah figure:

> but the deceiver is not the Christ. And when they reject him, he shall slay them with the sword, and there shall be many martyrs . . . And therefore those who die by his hand shall be martyrs, and shall be reckoned among the good and righteous martyrs who have pleased God in their life. (2)

Scholars of the text believe this to be a reference to Simon bar Kosiva, also known as Bar Kokhba (Aramaic for 'son of a star', referencing Numbers 24.17), who led a revolt in Jerusalem against Roman rule in 132–5 CE. According to the early Church Father Justin Martyr, Bar Kokhba executed Christians (presumably Jewish Christians) who did not join his cause (*First Apology* 31.6). If the identification of the false messiah as Bar Kokhba is correct, then the *Apocalypse of Peter* is a rather early apocryphal text and should be added to our evidence for Jewish Christianity. The text continues with Jesus showing Peter scenes of the end of the world in imagery reminiscent of John's apocalypse:

Cataracts of fire shall be let loose; and darkness and obscurity shall come up and clothe and veil the whole world; and the waters shall be changed and turned into coals of fire, and all that is in them shall burn, and the sea shall become fire. (5)

After the destruction, it is said, Jesus will come on the clouds with the angels, and the good will be rewarded.

Then comes the main act of the text: Jesus takes Peter on a gruesome tour of hell. Though important in Christian thought, hell is scarcely mentioned in the New Testament. Only the Tour of Hell apocalypses describe it in detail. In *Peter*, it is a dark, squalid place administered by the angels Uriel and Ezrael. The angels inflict a variety of punishments on the sinners, each one suited to their transgressions – blasphemers are hung by their tongues, women who adorned themselves to seduce men are hung by their hair, and the men who slept with them are hung by . . . well, I think you know where this is going. Murderers, idol worshippers, disobedient servants and children, child-killers, sorcerers – all the typical offenders – are punished, but special attention is paid to those who took part in the persecution of the author's community: those 'who caused the martyrs to die by their lying' (9) and 'the ones who had persecuted the righteous and delivered them up' (Greek v. 27). Of all the punishment scenes, the most alarming for modern readers are those addressing pre-marital sex and abortion. Girls who did not preserve their virginity until marriage have their flesh torn to pieces, and women who terminated their pregnancies are buried up to their necks in excrement. Their would-be children sit opposite them, striking their mothers with lightning that flashes out from their eyes. One can only wonder what effect this text would have had if it had been included in the canon. The apocalypse continues then with a brief view of the paradise that awaits the righteous, and finishes with Peter back at the Mount of Olives to witness the Transfiguration of Jesus.

Though the *Apocalypse of Peter* was lost for centuries, its impact continued to be felt through two texts that drew upon it for their own descriptions of the afterlife: the *Apocalypse of Paul* and the *Apocalypse of the Virgin*. *Paul* is available in numerous forms and languages, including Latin, Syriac, Coptic, Old Russian, and summaries in Greek. Likely it was composed in Greek in the early third century, though an introduction appended to some versions of the text places its origins at the end of the fourth. The story spins out of Paul's journey to the third heaven, mentioned in 2 Corinthians (12.2–4). Among the revelations given to Paul is the knowledge that each person, good or bad, has a guardian angel who relates daily to God all of his charge's evil works and continually directs the soul towards repentance. At death, the soul stands before God in judgement, and is sent to hell for its wickedness or to heaven for its righteousness.

The *Apocalypse of Paul* has had an enormous influence on western depictions of hell; its gruesome scenes appear in art and literature – including John Milton's *Paradise Lost* and Dante Alighieri's *Inferno* – and remain with us even today. In the East, the ninth-century *Apocalypse of the Virgin* conveyed the imagery of both *Peter* and *Paul* to new audiences. The text seems to have been very popular – numerous manuscripts exist in Greek, as well as Armenian, Ethiopic and Old Slavonic. Mary is accompanied on her tour of hell by Michael, the commander-in-chief of the angels. Given particular attention are punishments meted out to corrupt Church officials and those who habitually slept through church on Sundays.

The Tours of Hell are bleak, often crude, and macabre. Their depictions of punishment apparently were considered too unsettling for inclusion in the New Testament, but not for use in homilies, church decoration, and non-ecclesiastical art and literature. Modern readers of the tours also may take issue with their authors' decisions about who in their communities deserves eternal punishment, as well as how they are chastised. Take some consolation, however, in the fact that each of the authors, in his or her own way, also seems uncomfortable with the harsh judgements meted out to sinners. When Paul and Mary, joined by the angels and saints, plead for mercy on Christian sinners, Jesus grants wrongdoers relief from their punishments for a brief period – on Sundays in *Paul*, and for the 50 days of Pentecost in the *Virgin*. The Ethiopic version of the *Apocalypse of Peter* goes even further. Peter begs for mercy on sinners, and he is told that they will receive pardon. However, Peter is instructed not to reveal this to sinners because, knowing this, they might transgress even more. Punishment is not eternal after all. But, given the effectiveness of threats of eternal damnation, perhaps we should follow Peter and just keep that to ourselves.

Sources and studies

The apocalypses of Peter and Paul are found in J. K. Elliott, *The Apocryphal New Testament*, pp. 593–651. The *Apocalypse of the Virgin* was published by M. R. James in *Apocrypha Anecdota*, pp. 109–26; his translation also can be accessed online at the 'New Advent' site. The apocalypses of John can be found in John M. Court, *The Book of Revelation and the Johannine Apocalyptic Tradition*. For more on the Tour of Hell genre, see Martha Himmelfarb, *Tours of Hell*.

This brings us to the end of our discussion of Christian Apocrypha that focus specifically on the life and afterlife of Jesus. As with the material from Chapter 3, there is likely little in these texts that can be considered historical – at least not in the sense that these texts provide additional information about what *really* happened at Jesus' trial, or prove that the New Testament Gospels are wrong and Jesus did not *really* die on the cross, or deliver radically new teachings after his death. But the value of these texts lies not in what they say about Jesus, but in what they say about Christians, about how they used early Christian figures and events to discuss and debate new developments in the lives of their communities. Passion Narrative texts were written, at least in part, to work out relationships between Christians and Jews or between Christian groups with competing views of Jesus, post-resurrection dialogues were crafted to articulate Judaeo-Christian myths through Platonic cosmology, and Tour-of-Hell apocalypses were created to regulate Christian behaviour and encourage the faithful during times of turmoil. Certainly Jesus appears in these texts – and in interesting, sometimes provocative, ways – but not the historical Jesus; nor, for that matter, does the genuine Pontius Pilate appear, or the real Mary Magdalene. The only real people in these texts are their authors and readers. Their imaginative stories about Jesus offer us a window into the real experiences of Christians in different places and times. The copyists and translators of these texts also believed the texts to be important, speaking to them in ways the canonical texts did not. Some modern readers may feel the same.

But enough, for now, about Jesus. There are more apocryphal texts for us to examine, these ones featuring stories of other early Christian figures, including the apostles, Jesus' mother and father, John the Baptist, and others. Unfortunately, these texts receive far less attention from scholars and in popular culture than the apocryphal gospels, but they are no less fascinating. So don't stop reading now. There are more secret scriptures to reveal.

5

After Jesus: legends of
the early Church

The apocryphal texts we have examined so far focus primarily on the life of Jesus, from his birth to his early resurrection appearances. The texts are similar in many ways to the canonical Gospels, which also present tales of Jesus, and to Revelation, in which Jesus takes John on a visionary journey. But the New Testament contains more than Gospels and apocalypses. The four canonical Gospels are followed by the Acts of the Apostles, an account of the early years of the Church following Jesus' death, and an assortment of letters, by Paul, Peter, James, Jude and John. These texts also have counterparts among the Christian Apocrypha in tales of the missionary journeys of individual apostles and in additional letters not found in the New Testament. Among the Apocrypha also are tales of other figures in Jesus' life, such as his mother Mary, his father Joseph, Mary Magdalene and John the Baptist. The texts provide readers with biographical information absent from the New Testament. But, as with the gospel materials, the goal of the texts is never simply to 'fill in' gaps. Some of them aim also to establish or promote devotional sites where pilgrims can view the saints' remains. Others are written to support or establish points of Christian doctrine, such as the assumption of the Virgin Mary, body and soul, into heaven. And still others portray their subjects as embodying the beliefs and practices of their communities – beliefs and practices that eventually were declared heretical and are known today only because the texts somehow survived destruction.

Legends and writings of the apostles

According to the canonical book of Acts, Jesus finished his 40 days of post-resurrection teaching and then sent the apostles off on their missionary journeys. Though most of the Acts focuses on the exploits of Peter and Paul, some of the text's more memorable stories feature the apostle Philip. In Acts 8.4–25, Philip preaches in Samaria and encounters a local magician named Simon – known usually by the name Simon Magus, or Simon the magician. Peter and John come to Samaria at Philip's request and bestow upon the community the power of the Holy Spirit. Simon offers the apostles money in exchange for this power but is rebuffed for his 'simony'. This is Simon's ultimate legacy: his name synonymous with the sin of paying for sacraments or positions in the Church. As we will see, the apocryphal writers have much more to say about Simon, but in Acts his story ends with him repenting of his offence. Then Philip is spirited away to a desert road where he converts and baptizes an Ethiopian eunuch (Acts 8.26–40). After this interlude, Acts shifts its focus to Paul, and the text finishes with the apostle preaching in Rome.

It has long been suspected that the author of Acts constructed his text based on oral or written tales of the apostles. Perhaps these same sources contributed to other accounts of the apostles' activities found principally in a body of texts known as the 'apocryphal acts'. The apocryphal acts report the missionary activities of individual apostles in places assigned to them for evangelization by Jesus. Various sources mention this apportioning of duties; the earliest is Origen, whose account also includes some information that may be derived from the apocryphal acts:

> The holy apostles and disciples of our Saviour were scattered over the whole world. Thomas, tradition tells us, was chosen for Parthia, Andrew for Scythia, John for Asia, where he remained till his death at Ephesus. Peter seems to have preached in Pontus, Galatia and Bithynia, Cappadocia and Asia, to the Jews of the Dispersion. Finally he came to Rome where he was crucified, head downwards at his own request. What need be said of Paul, who from Jerusalem as far as Illyricum preached in all its fullness the gospel of Christ, and later was martyred in Rome under Nero?
>
> (Eusebius, *Ecclesiastical History* 3.1,
> appealing to Origen's *Commentary on Genesis* 3)

When they reach their destinations, the apostles preach, convert, work miracles, battle magicians, encounter conflict, and ultimately meet their ends, usually through martyrdom. The five earliest apocryphal acts – those of John, Paul, Peter, Andrew and Thomas – were written in the late second to early third century. Despite the popularity of the acts, representatives of proto-orthodox and orthodox Christianity seem to have had an uneasy relationship with the tales. Early writers seemed comfortable with them; indeed, the *Acts of Paul* even came close to being considered canonical in some areas, and a portion of the text, *3 Corinthians*, was included in the Bibles of eastern churches for centuries. But by the fourth century, orthodox Christianity either edited the apocryphal acts to omit objectionable content or reduced them to just 'martyr-doms'. Thanks to the orthodox pruning of the apocryphal acts, reconstructing the original texts can be very difficult. Today, only the *Acts of Thomas* exists in full.

The origins of the apocryphal acts are somewhat mysterious. They do not seem dependent on the canonical Acts, nor are they clearly dependent on one another; yet they share certain common literary and theological elements. In many ways they resemble ancient Greek and Roman novels. Like today's novels, the Graeco-Roman novels are essentially lengthy narratives; they developed and enjoyed their heyday in the first to fourth centuries CE. One of the best-known novels is the *Life of Apollonius of Tyana* by Flavius Philostratus, which tells the story of a real-life wandering philosopher and wonder worker of the first century. The apocryphal acts, too, recount the teachings and activities of historical miracle-workers; but thematically they have more in common with a subgenre of the novel known as 'romances'. The romances, such as Chariton's *Callirhoe* and Longus's *Daphnis and Chloe*, follow a stereotypical structure: two young protagonists are separated and then later reunited after a series of adventures and journeys; through it all they remain chaste and faithful to one another. In the apocryphal acts, however, the theme of the romances is inverted: the apostles interact with young women, but there is no consummation; instead, the women deny their former romantic partners and join the apostles in a life of chastity. Looked at another way, the acts can be seen as classic love triangles, with a ruler (representing society) vying for the affections of a woman with another man, the apostle (representing Christianity and/or Jesus).

The theology behind the apocryphal acts is represented in the apostle who lives an ascetic life and advocates celibacy for everyone. This lifestyle may have little attraction to modern readers, but what remains appealing are the important roles played by women in the texts. At times, the women, not the apostles, are the stars of the acts. This has led some commentators to argue that the apocryphal acts were written by and perhaps even for women, to demonstrate how conversion to ascetic Christianity could bring liberation from the restrictive expectations placed on women in societies of the time. It's an intriguing possibility, but other scholars see the female characters as the least important element of the love triangle – the real drama is the conflict that takes place between the apostles and the rulers, between the sacred powers and the secular authorities.

There is not sufficient space here to discuss all of the apocryphal acts and their numerous medieval revisions. Many of these revisions are not even available in English translations. We will focus our discussion instead on three of the five early apocryphal acts, along with stories of Judas, and some other texts related to the apostles. The activities of the remaining six apostles are recorded in their own acts or martyrdoms, though these texts have attracted far less interest from scholars because they were written somewhat later than the five early apocryphal acts. Some of the later acts, along with orthodox revisions of the early acts, also circulated as a group in the popular Latin collection known as the *Apostolic History* attributed to Abdias, the first bishop of Babylon, and in the Ethiopic–Arabic *Contendings of the Apostles*. Several well-known disciples of the apostles – including Mark, Luke, Timothy and Titus – also star in their own texts, as do a few prominent members of the Church introduced in the canonical Acts: Matthias, Barnabas, Stephen and Ananias.

Sources and studies

For a recent and comprehensive survey of the literature, see Hans-Josef Klauck, *The Apocryphal Acts of the Apostles*. The translations used in the following discussion are from J. K. Elliott, *The Apocryphal New*

Testament, pp. 229–533, unless otherwise noted. On women as composers of the apocryphal acts see Stevan L. Davies, *The Revolt of the Widows* and Virginia Burrus, *Chastity as Autonomy*. Summaries of the later apocryphal acts are found in J. K. Elliott, *The Apocryphal New Testament*, pp. 512–33 and Hans-Josef Klauck, *The Apocryphal Acts*, pp. 231–53.

The *Acts of John*

The *Acts of John* is an ideal place to start our investigation of the apocryphal acts because it is indicative of the style and interests of the corpus as well as the difficulties involved in studying them. Originally the *Acts of John* was about as long as the Gospel of Matthew, but now only two-thirds of it survives. Scholars have cobbled together its contents from a variety of sources. These include a fourth-century fragment from the Oxyrhynchus Papyri (P.Oxy. 850), a handful of Greek manuscripts of isolated stories, and numerous manuscripts in multiple languages of the conclusion to the text: John's *metastasis* (or 'departure' from life; unlike the other apostles, John did not die a martyr). There is still uncertainty as to the ordering of the materials; for example, chapters originally numbered 87 to 105, found in only one Greek manuscript, are now believed to have once stood between 36 and 37.

Several stories within the *Acts of John* reflect the apocryphal acts' interest in celibacy. In the first story (chs 48—54), a young farmer kills his father for warning him not to sleep with the wife of a fellow labourer. In despair over his crime, the farmer prepares to kill the woman, her husband and himself. Then the apostle John appears on the scene. John restores the young man's father to life, but the farmer, still seeking revenge on the object of his lust, cuts off his genitals and throws them at the woman. John then admonishes him for such an extreme response, saying it is not his genitals that were the source of his problems but his passions.

In the second story (chs 60—61), John and his companions stay overnight at an inn. To his dismay, John's bed is infested with bedbugs. He commands the bugs to leave his bed and they do so, gathering in the corner of the room until he commands them to return to the bed in the morning. How is this story about celibacy? Well, in Greek the words for 'bug' and 'girl' are very similar to one another; an astute reader of the text in Greek would recognize that the story is really about John ordering women from his bed.

Finally, the third story (chs 62—86) introduces us to Callimachus, who covets John's companion Drusiana. When Drusiana became Christian, she refused to sleep with her husband Andronicus. In response, he locked her up in a tomb saying, 'Either I'll have you as a wife, as I had you before, or you must die!' (63). Fortunately, Drusiana was able to persuade Andronicus to adopt Christianity and celibacy just as she did. But now Drusiana must deal with the advances of a second man, Callimachus. Distraught over having brought him to sin, Drusiana dies of grief. Undaunted, Callimachus persuades Andronicus's steward Fortunatus to help him gain access to Drusiana's tomb so that he can defile her body. Later, John and his other companions arrive and see Fortunatus slain by a serpent. Callimachus, though, has repented of his sins after encountering an angel who came to protect Drusiana's body. The story finishes with John raising Drusiana to life; in turn she raises Fortunatus, but he refuses to repent and eventually succumbs to the poison of the snake bite.

Another major section of the text (chs 87—105) features a dialogue between John and Drusiana about Jesus. This section bears a distinctly Docetic flavour – that is, Jesus is portrayed as only 'appearing' (from the Greek *dokeo*) to be human. John narrates the time when he and his brother James were called by Jesus to join his ministry. At first John sees Jesus as a man 'fair and comely, and of a cheerful countenance' (88), but James sees him as a child. Later, Jesus appears to John as a man, bald-headed with a thick and flowing beard, but to James as a youth whose beard is just starting. This polymorphic ('many-formed') portrayal of Jesus is confusing to John, but it clearly demonstrates to the reader that Jesus is not like normal humans. Indeed, Jesus is said to never close his eyes nor leave footprints; he is even ghostlike – John says, 'sometimes when I meant to touch him, I met a material and solid body; and at other times again when

I felt him, the substance was immaterial and bodiless and as if it were not existing at all' (93). Polymorphic depictions of Christ are not unique to the *Acts of John*; the motif occurs in a number of texts from the Christian Apocrypha, including the *Acts of Peter*, the *Gospel of Judas*, the *Secret Book of John* and the *Revelation of the Magi*.

Next follows the most fascinating portion of the text: a rival account of the Passion of Jesus. The events take place before Jesus' arrest. Jesus is with the apostles, and he asks them to join him in a hymn. The hymn is mostly a series of contradictory statements, followed by the audience's response of 'Amen' – for example,

> I will flee and I will stay; I will adorn, and I will be adorned; I will be united, and I will unite; I have no house, and I have houses; I have no place, and I have places; I have no temple, and I have temples.
>
> (95)

The meaning of the hymn becomes clear after Jesus' arrest. Having fled along with the other disciples, John hides in a cave at the Mount of Olives. There Jesus appears to him, bathed in light, and says,

> John, to the multitude down below in Jerusalem I am being crucified, and pierced with lances and reeds, and gall and vinegar is given me to drink. But to you I am speaking, and pay attention to what I say.
>
> (97)

What follows is a description of the cross, not as the physical instrument of Jesus' death, but as the symbolic 'cross of light . . . which has united all things by the Word' (98—99). And the body that hangs upon that wooden cross is not truly Jesus. So, he can both suffer and suffer not, be hanged and not hang. Only John is given this knowledge, and Jesus warns him that others will not understand: 'I was reckoned to be what I am not, not being what I was to many others; but they will call me something else, which is vile and not worthy of me' (99). It is tempting to see behind this section of the text evidence of the conflict partially visible in the canonical letters of John, which discuss a division in the community that led to the departure of certain members who refused to confess that 'Jesus Christ [had] come in the flesh' (1 John 4.2–3;

and 2 John 7). The *Acts of John* and the canonical epistles can be seen, perhaps, as the products of two groups of Christians branching out from the community behind the Gospel of John, each having their own particular views about the divinity of Jesus. The full-blown Gnosticism of the *Apocryphon of John*, discussed in the previous chapter, may reflect a further stage in the development of the *Acts of John*'s Docetic view of Jesus.

The *Acts of Paul*

Paul, the famous letter writer of the New Testament and self-professed apostle to the Gentiles, is well represented in the Christian Apocrypha, though not always in flattering ways. His evangelizing activities are narrated in the *Acts of Paul*, the earliest attested of the apocryphal acts. It is mentioned by Tertullian around 200 CE, and both Origen and Hippolytus (*c.* 204) quote from it without any sense of it being heretical. Even in the fourth century some Christians continued to value the text; this is reflected by Eusebius, who considers the *Acts of Paul* a 'spurious' writing (along with the *Shepherd of Hermas* and the *Apocalypse of Peter*), but not heretical. Like the *Acts of John*, much of the *Acts of Paul* is now lost. What remains are principally three large units which also circulated independently of each other: the *Acts of Paul and Thecla*, the Corinthian Correspondence (featuring *3 Corinthians*), and Paul's martyrdom. The theme of the text, as with the other apocryphal acts, is sexual abstinence. It infuses virtually every episode of the text and is the substance of Paul's preaching. There is some basis for Paul's interest in abstinence in his authentic letters – in 1 Corinthians he writes that it is best that Christians not marry, but if they are married, that they live as if they were not (1 Corinthians 7). In the *Acts*, however, sexual continence is so important that resurrection is promised as a reward specifically to those who keep themselves pure.

The *Acts of Paul and Thecla* is perhaps the best-known story of all the apocryphal acts. That is because its portrayal of the virgin Thecla, who baptizes and preaches as an apostle, offers tantalizing evidence for a form of early Christianity in which women had important roles, roles denied women even in some modern churches. If the available manuscripts are any indication, *Thecla* enjoyed great popularity in antiquity – we have 80 Greek manuscripts, four Latin versions, and translations into eastern languages. And throughout medieval times, Thecla, as the first woman martyr, was a much venerated saint.

Thecla's story begins when Paul, accompanied by Demas and Hermogenes (mentioned as opponents of the faith in 2 Timothy 4.10 and 1.15), enter the city of Iconium. Paul begins to preach and, in a series of beatitudes, he imparts his teaching on sexual abstinence:

> blessed are those who have kept the flesh chaste, for they shall become a temple of God; blessed are the continent, for God shall speak with them . . . blessed are those who have wives as not having them, for they shall experience God. (3.5)

Thecla is entranced by Paul's words. But her mother Theoclia and her fiancé Thamyris worry about the effect these teachings are having on her. Through the scheming of Demas and Hermogenes, Thamyris manipulates the city's proconsul to imprison Paul. Undaunted, Thecla visits Paul by night. When she is discovered, she is brought before the proconsul, who condemns her to be burned at the stake. Paul, on the other hand, is merely flogged and expelled from the city. Thecla needs to die as an example to other women who refuse to fulfil their appointed roles in Iconium society – to obey and care for parents, and to marry and be submissive to husbands. So disruptive is Thecla to order in Iconium that her own mother bursts out, 'Burn the wicked one; burn her who will not marry in the midst of the theatre, that all the women who have been taught by this man may be afraid' (3.20). But God has other plans for Thecla. At the last moment, Thecla is saved from the fire by a miraculous torrent of rain and hail.

Thecla rejoins Paul and together they journey to Antioch. There an influential citizen named Alexander becomes enamoured with her. Thecla refuses him and humiliates him in public by tearing his cloak and pulling off his crown. For this she is sent before the governor, who condemns her to die in the arena in battle against the beasts. But in Antioch, unlike her native Iconium, the women call out to Thecla in support, and even some of the female animals refuse to harm her. The climax of the battle comes when Thecla throws herself into a pool of water filled with seals; there she baptizes herself and then a bolt of lightning kills the seals. Further attempts to kill Thecla fail until finally Alexander begs the governor to set her free. Thecla meets up with Paul again and he commissions her to preach the gospel. Her missionary journeys first take her to Iconium where she makes peace with her mother and discovers that her former fiancé Thamyris has died. Thecla then travels to Seleucia where tradition says she lived as an ascetic for 72 years.

The conflict over the roles of women in the *Acts of Paul and Thecla* had real-life consequences. Tertullian shows disdain for the text because women were appealing to it to defend their right to teach and baptize (*Baptism* 17). He reveals also that the author of the *Acts* was an elder, or presbyter, in Asia who wrote the text in Tertullian's day in order to add to the prestige of Paul. As punishment, the presbyter was removed from office. *Thecla* also may reflect discussion about women's roles in the Church from as far back as the early second century. The canonical Pastoral Epistles (1 and 2 Timothy, and Titus) defend the traditional roles of women, encouraging them to be submissive to their husbands, love their children and be good managers of the household (see particularly Titus 2.3–5). Were the Pastoral letters written in reaction to the *Acts of Paul and Thecla*? If so, the Asian presbyter must be considered a compiler of earlier stories of Paul, not their author. If not, certainly they react to a similar point of view that calls for women to be allowed to participate more actively in the Church.

Scholars interested in the Christian Apocrypha's proto-feminist portrayals of women or their positive female imagery are frequently cautioned by critics that the texts very likely had no bearing on Christian practice and relationships. But in *Thecla* we have that much sought-after concrete example of a text that was written and used by Christians to argue for expanded choices for women in society and some level of equality between men and women in Christian communities.

Paul's renown as a writer of letters does not go ignored by writers of the Christian Apocrypha. An episode in the *Acts of Paul* set in Corinth includes a copy of a letter that Paul is said to have written to the community. In the story, two men, Simon and Cleobius, come to Corinth saying,

There is no resurrection of the flesh but only of the spirit, and the body of man is not created by God, and God did not create the world and does not know the world, nor has Jesus Christ been crucified but only in appearance, and he was not born of Mary nor of the seed of David. (8)

Disturbed by this new teaching, the Corinthians send a letter to Paul at Philippi seeking his guidance. Paul's response counters Simon and Cleobius's Gnostic theology with standard proto-orthodox teachings. The letter, like the *Acts of Paul and Thecla*, circulated independently of the *Acts of Paul*. Some churches, in Syria and Armenia, even included it in their Bibles as *3 Corinthians*.

Also sometimes included in Bibles alongside the canonical letters of Paul is an *Epistle to the Laodiceans*. The letter was composed between the second and fourth centuries in Greek but now exists only in Latin and European vernaculars. Surprisingly, it appears also in a few Latin New Testament manuscripts from the sixth and eighth centuries and was even included in John Wycliffe's English Bible from the fourteenth century. A 'letter from Laodicea' is mentioned at the end of the canonical letter to the Colossians (Colossians 4.16). The original letter to the Laodiceans, if it ever truly existed, is now lost, but a later writer made up for this loss with the apocryphal *Epistle to the Laodiceans*, created by cobbling together phrases found in Philippians and Galatians.

Also included among the Pauline Apocrypha are the *Epistles of Paul and Seneca*, a series of 14 letters exchanged by Paul and the first-century Roman moralist. Jerome was convinced of their authenticity, and so they were regarded down to the Renaissance. But they appear to date from the fourth century. For a conversation between two great thinkers, the *Epistles* are rather disappointing. Most of the time the writers simply exchange compliments and declarations of friendship. In one letter, Seneca writes of Paul's letters, 'they are so lofty and so brilliant with noble sentiments that in my opinion generations of men could hardly be enough to become established and perfected in them' (1). Seneca tells Paul he has read his letters to Nero, who 'was amazed that one whose education had not been normal could have such ideas' (7).

The apocryphal Pauline letters stand out among the Christian Apocrypha because of their semi-canonical status. But they were afforded this status primarily because the letters are so consistent with proto-orthodox theology. Indeed, it's hard to take offence at them when they do very little but parrot statements found in Paul's canonical letters. Keep in mind, though, that the author of the *Acts of Paul and Thecla* and authors of other unorthodox Pauline apocrypha also saw a consistency between their views and those of their beloved apostle. Paul's views on such issues as resurrection and celibacy are often contradictory or at least sufficiently ambiguous that they can be developed in multiple directions. The inconsistent portrayals of Paul in apocryphal texts derive ultimately from Paul's own inconsistencies of thought.

Sources and studies

For a discussion of the interplay between the *Acts of Paul* and the Pastoral Epistles, see Dennis R. MacDonald, *The Legend and the Apostle*. To read other Pauline apocrypha, see the *Revelation of Paul* and the *Prayer of the Apostle Paul* in Marvin Meyer, *The Nag Hammadi Scriptures*, pp. 15–18, 313–19.

The *Acts of Peter*

As the rock upon which the Church is built (Matthew 16.18), Peter holds a prominent place among the apostles, and is thus the subject of numerous apocryphal texts that record his activities and his teachings. In many of them, Peter battles Simon Magus, the Samaritan magician from Acts 8, in miracle contests to determine who is the true God – Simon or Jesus. In other texts, Peter clashes with his fellow apostle Paul to determine who preaches the true gospel.

Like other apocryphal acts, the *Acts of Peter* is today incomplete; what we have of the text is reconstructed from a number of disparate sources. The most important of these is a sixth-/seventh-century Latin translation known by scholars as the *Actus Vercellenses*, which preserves about two-thirds of the *Acts* but seems to have changed the original text's theme to reflect a problem encountered by Christians in the third and fourth centuries: the forgiveness of those who leave the faith at times of persecution but wish to return. The original interests of the *Acts of Peter*, which accord with the other apocryphal acts, can be observed in our other sources for the text: the martyrdom from three Greek manuscripts and numerous translations (in Coptic, Syriac, Georgian, Armenian, Slavonic, Arabic and Ethiopic), a single *Act of Peter* in Coptic from the fifth-century Bruce Codex, and a Greek fragment of chapters 25 and 26 in Papyrus Oxyrhynchus 849, dated to the late third or fourth century. Additionally, the Greek *Life of St Abercius*, from the fourth century, recycles speeches and stories from the *Acts of Peter* as episodes in the life of Abercius, a second-century bishop of Hierapolis.

The main drama of the text is a miracle contest between Peter and Simon Magus. The canonical Acts says little – and little that is flattering – about Simon, but other Christian sources reveal more about his life and teachings. Justin Martyr (*First Apology* 26.2; see also Irenaeus, *Against Heresies* 1.23.1–4), himself a former native of Samaria, says that Simon came from the Samaritan village of Gitta and was active in Rome in the reign of Claudius (41–54 CE). The Samaritans in Rome worshipped him as the 'First God' and his companion Helene was considered his 'First Thought', a term in Gnostic literature for a being that represents the creative power of God and, at the same time, functions as his consort. Justin tells also of a statue on the Tiber River bearing the inscription 'to the holy god Simon'. This statue was found by archaeologists in the sixteenth century but Justin had the inscription wrong – it actually reads 'to the faithful god Semo Sanco', a Roman deity. Someone, either Justin or Simon's followers or someone else, wilfully or accidentally misread the inscription. The *Acts of Peter*, like the canonical Acts, shows no interest in the historical Simon's teachings; he is used in these texts essentially to prove the superiority of Christianity over other religious systems of the day.

The lost early chapters of the *Acts of Peter* may have contained an expansion of the story of Simon from Acts (recounted in summary, it seems, in ch. 17). Apparently, in this new telling of the tale, Simon was not so repentant of his attempt at simony and now he has come to Rome to attract new followers. When Peter arrives, he challenges Simon to confront him in battle. They meet in the forum where the people of Rome pay high fees for a chance to see this contest of champions. They challenge Peter to outperform Simon, shouting,

> Show us, Peter, who your god is or which majesty it is which gave you such confidence . . . We have had evidence from Simon, let us have yours also; show us, both of you, whom we must believe.   (23)

Ultimately, Peter wins the contest and the crowd calls for Simon's death. Surprisingly, Peter won't allow it. Harkening back to the *Actus Vercellenses*' theme of forgiveness, Peter says in Simon's defence, 'For should even he repent, it is better. For God will not remember the evil' (28). But forgiveness is clearly not the theme of the original text, for in a summary chapter (32) in the martyrdom, Simon meets his end at Peter's hand. According to the story, Simon returns to Rome and demonstrates his ability to fly. Worried that the believers would once again abandon Christ and follow Simon, Peter prays, 'let him fall down and become crippled but not die, let him be disabled and break his leg in three places' (32). And fall he does. Simon's followers carry him off to Aricia where, following an operation, Simon dies of his injuries.

The martyrdom of Peter features the theme of celibacy so prevalent in other apocryphal acts, as well as typically unorthodox teachings. Peter is arrested for encouraging his converts to abandon intercourse. At his own request, Peter is crucified upside down to reflect the backward nature of the world, which sees 'the ugly as beautiful and the really evil as good' (38). The remedy for this situation is found in a saying of Jesus found also in the *Gospel of Thomas*; Peter says,

> Concerning this the Lord says in a mystery, 'Unless you make the right as the left and the left as the right, and the top as the bottom and the front as the back, you shall not know the Kingdom.'
>   (38; cf. *Gospel of Thomas* 22)

The conflict between Peter and Simon is told also in several other apocryphal texts. The most interesting of these by far is the *Pseudo-Clementine Romance*, where Simon is portrayed in many ways very much like the apostle Paul. *Pseudo-Clement* is named for the prominence in the text of Clement, a successor to Peter as Bishop of Rome and the author of *1 Clement* from the Apostolic Fathers. The sources for the text are quite complicated and scholars have yet to reach consensus on how they relate to each other and how they originated. There are two main versions: the *Homilies*, a collection of 20 sermons of Peter in Greek, and the *Recognitions*, a ten-book narrative translated into Latin by Rufinus of Aquileia around 407 CE. The two are believed to go back to a common Jewish-Christian source written in Syria in the third century.

The framework of the original text documents Clement's interactions with Peter along with some details of Clement's earlier life. In a letter appended to the *Homilies*, Clement informs James that Peter has died and that Clement has been appointed his successor. Attached to the letter is 'Clement's Epitome of the Popular Sermons of Peter', which forms the bulk of the text. As Clement describes the activities and teachings of Peter, he tells also the tale of his own family's separation and reunion – the 'romance' of the title. Shortly after Clement's birth, his mother Mattidia had a vision warning her that, if she did not leave Rome immediately with her twin sons (Faustinus and Faustinianus), all of her family would die. They head off to Athens and are never heard from again. When Clement turns 12, his father Faustus sets out to sea in search of his wife and sons; then he too goes missing.

Clement grows to adulthood, becomes interested in Christianity and joins Peter on his journeys from town to town in pursuit of Simon. In *Pseudo-Clement*, Peter's encounters with Simon are less miracle contests than wars of words; but through these disputes we learn much about the beliefs of the Jewish Christians who composed the text. We also discover some additional details of Simon's life, including the story of his birth, his time spent in Egypt learning magic, and his association with John the Baptist – Simon is said to have been second-in-command to John, and became leader of the group after John's death, before leaving to gather his own followers. In the course of the narrative, two former followers of Simon are revealed to be Clement's lost brothers, and the three are reunited eventually with their mother and father.

The Jewish-Christian origin of *Pseudo-Clement* adds weight to the theory that Peter's opponent in the text, though named as Simon, is really Paul, an apostle often vilified in Jewish-Christian texts. In one of Peter's disputes with Simon (*Homilies* 17.13–19), Peter diminishes Simon's interpretation of Jesus because the knowledge was granted to him only in a vision. Peter, on the other hand, knew Jesus when he was alive. Peter asks,

> Can anyone be made competent to teach through a vision? And if your opinion is, 'That is possible,' why then did our teacher spend a whole year with us who were awake? . . . But if you were visited by him for the space of an hour and were instructed by him and thereby have become an apostle, then proclaim his words, expound what he has taught, be a friend to his apostles and do not contend with me, who am his confidant; for you have in hostility withstood me, who am a firm rock, the foundation stone of the church.
>
> (*Homilies* 17.19.1,4)

Paul, too, only knew Jesus from visions (see Galatians 1.15–17; Acts 9.3–6); so it is tempting to see Peter's criticism here as an attack on the apostle to the Gentiles. As further proof, scholars point to Peter's words in the *Epistle of Peter to James* that begins the *Homilies*:

> For some from among the Gentiles have rejected my lawful preaching and have preferred a lawless and absurd doctrine of the man who is my enemy. And indeed some have attempted, whilst I am still alive, to distort my words by interpretations of many sorts, as if I taught the dissolution of the law and, although I was of this opinion, did not express it openly.
>
> (*Homilies* 2.3–4; cf. Paul's criticism of Peter in Galatians 2.11–14)

Pseudo-Clement is not our only evidence of Jewish-Christian antipathy towards Paul. Several early Christian groups, who followed at least some Jewish practices, also spoke out against Paul. According to the bishop Epiphanius, the Ebionites, who many scholars believe composed *Pseudo-Clement*, circulated 'trumped-up charges of evildoing and deceit' against the apostle (*Refutation of all Heresies* 30.16.6–9). Another text showing Peter at odds with Paul is the *Book of the Rolls*. The text, likely of Syrian origin, contains a mixture of material composed before and after the Arab conquest of Egypt in the seventh century. Among the older materials is an account of several miracle contests between Paul and Peter. Though Paul later reveals he only contended with Peter to orchestrate conversions to Christianity, Peter instructs his disciple Clement to guard his teachings from Paul. He says to him, 'As God lives no one ought to divulge these mysteries to Paul [or be he Paul] or those who resemble him' (p. 405), and goes on to describe Paul as the one 'who had tampered with the language of the books' (p. 406).

The conflicts between Peter and Paul in the Christian Apocrypha may seem shocking given how well the two seem to get along in the canonical Acts. Peter even comes to the defence of Paul when the Jerusalem church questions his mission to the Gentiles (Acts 15.7–11). But even the canonical New Testament shows occasional signs of tension in their relationship. For example, in the letter to the Galatians, Paul expresses anger at Peter for refusing to eat with the Gentile Christians of Antioch (Galatians 2.11–14) and thereby causing a rift in Antioch's Christian community. By the time of composition of *Pseudo-Clement* and the *Book of the Rolls*, Jewish Christians were an ever-shrinking minority in the Church and, declared heretics by the more powerful Gentile majority, were eventually persecuted out of existence. It should come as no surprise after all, then, to find evidence of Jewish Christians fighting back against orthodox persecution, though surreptitiously, through texts in which Peter, their apostolic champion, battles and defeats the apostle to the Gentiles with his superior teachings and divine might.

Sources and studies: There is no current, complete English translation of the lengthy *Pseudo-Clementine Romance*. For now, the translation from the Ante-Nicene Fathers collection can be read online at the 'Compassionate Spirit' website. To read more about the Jewish-Christian origins of the text see F. Stanley Jones, *An Ancient Jewish Christian Source on the History of Christianity*; and for additional information about Simon Magus see Birger A. Pearson, *Ancient Gnosticism*, pp. 26–33. Other Petrine apocrypha not discussed here include the *Acts of Peter and the Twelve Apostles* (in Marvin Meyer, *The Nag Hammadi Scriptures*, p. 357–66) and the *Preaching of Peter* (also known as the *Kerygma Petri*, an early second-century text available only in excerpts provided by Clement of Alexandria and Origen; see pp. 34–41 in Wilhelm Schneemelcher's *New Testament Apocrypha* collection). The *Book of the Rolls* (also known under the titles *Clement* and the *Apocalypse of Peter*) is available in Garshuni and Ethiopic. For a translation of the Garshuni text, see Alphonse Mingana, 'Apocalypse of Peter'.

The *Life of Judas*

Judas, the infamous betrayer of Jesus, does not have his own acts and martyrdom texts. Unlike the other apostles, Judas did not die with honour after a glorious career of preaching and performing miracles. Instead, he met a gruesome end, either at his own hand by hanging (Matthew 27.1–10) or by falling and splitting open (Acts 1.16–20). A third account of Judas's death attributed to Papias of Hierapolis (*Exposition of the Sayings of the Lord*, Book 4, fragment 4, as reported by Apollinaris of Laodicaea) says he became bloated with disease, so much that 'his genitals appeared more loathsome and larger than anyone else's, and when he relieved himself there passed through it pus and worms from every part of his body, much to his shame'. Eventually, he died from the agony. Other traditions about Judas appear in a range of apocryphal texts discussed already (the Syriac *Life of the Blessed Virgin Mary*, the *Book of the Cock*, the *Gospel of Judas*, *Narrative of Joseph of Arimathea*, and the *Descent into Hell*). Further details of Judas's life are provided in two additional texts.

A full *Life of Judas* is found in a number of Greek and Latin manuscripts as well as versions in European and Slavic languages, none dating earlier than the twelfth century. Though rarely mentioned by Church writers, the *Life of Judas* was extremely popular as folk literature, appearing in incunabula (early printed books), and incorporated into plays and *The Golden Legend*. The story draws on motifs from the biblical story of Moses and from the Greek myth of Oedipus, who unknowingly killed his birth father and married his mother. Judas's parents are named Reuben and Ciborea. On the night of Judas's conception, Ciborea has a dream in which she is told that she will give birth to a child who will destroy the people. Reuben and Ciborea cannot bring themselves to kill Judas, so they place him in a basket and send him out to sea. The basket lands in Scarioth where the queen of the country raises him as her own child. Judas reaches adulthood, kills the queen's son, and then flees to Jerusalem where he enters the employ of Pilate. In the course of his duties he meets up again with Reuben and slays him. Pilate then gives Judas all of Reuben's property and his wife. One day Ciborea mentions to Judas how she had placed her son in the sea. Horrified, they realize they are mother and son.

At Ciborea's suggestion, Judas goes to Jesus for redemption, becomes one of the Twelve, and later betrays Jesus and dies.

The second apocryphal Judas text focuses on the origins and transmission of the coins paid to Judas to betray Jesus. The *Legend of the Thirty Pieces of Silver* is found in two main forms: a western version in Latin translated also into several European languages, and an eastern version in Syriac, found also incorporated into Solomon of Basra's chronicle the *Book of the Bee*. Both the Latin and Syriac versions likely derive from a lost Greek original written sometime before the twelfth century. The theme of the *Legend* is fate. For 2,000 years, the coins stay together as a unit and are providentially guided to their ultimate goal. They begin as the creation of Abraham's father Terah, are used to buy a burial plot for Abraham and Sarah, are paid to the sons of Jacob in the sale of their brother Joseph, are later deposited in Solomon's Temple, and with its fall, are taken to Babylon during the exile. From Babylon, the coins make their way eventually to Judaea where the Jewish leaders use them to pay Judas to betray Jesus. Finally, the coins are used to purchase the potter's field where Judas is buried (mentioned in Matthew 27.6–8; Acts 1.18–19). Gold Judas coins, not silver, were popular relics in the Middle Ages. This transformation from silver to gold is explained in some versions of the *Legend*. It's an interesting feature, because it allows owners of the gold Judas coins to become part of the story, to believe that their ownership or stewardship of the holy object is also providentially ordained.

Sources and studies

For the *Life of Judas*, see Paull Franklin Baum, 'The Mediaeval Legend of Judas Iscariot'. The western versions of the *Legend of the Thirty Pieces of Silver* are surveyed in George F. Hill, 'The Thirty Pieces of Silver'. The excerpt from Papias can be found in Michael W. Holmes, *The Apostolic Fathers*, pp. 583–5.

Other people in the life of Jesus

The apostles are not the only characters from the canonical Gospels featured in the Christian Apocrypha. We have seen already in

119

previous chapters that Mary Magdalene, John the Baptist, and Jesus' parents, Mary and Joseph, appear here and there as part of the Jesus biography, particularly in the *Protevangelium of James* and in Gnostic–mystical texts like the *Gospel of Mary* and the *Pistis Sophia*. Additional texts exist that individually focus on these figures, providing additional biographical material and information relating to their veneration as saints.

The *Dormition of Mary*

Just as Christians composed stories establishing an origin suitable for the mother of God's Son, they created also a text that brings Mary's tale to an appropriate conclusion. Actually, they produced numerous texts on this subject – depending on how scholars tabulate the evidence, there are somewhere between 30 and 64 texts about Mary's death. Though they go by different titles (the best known is the *Dormition* [or 'falling asleep'] *of Mary*) and differ considerably in their contents, they essentially reflect two approaches to granting Mary a dignified end: either Mary dies and after three days she is taken body and soul into paradise, or Mary dies and her body remains on earth awaiting reunion with her soul at the end of time. Both approaches originated in the fifth century and gave rise, many centuries later, to the Vatican's dogma of the Virgin's bodily Assumption – meaning that Mary ascended body and soul to heaven just like her Son.

Scholars of the *Dormition* divide the traditions into two categories: the Bethlehem tradition, in which some of the story takes place at Mary's house in Bethlehem, and the Palm tradition, in which a palm from the Tree of Life plays a large part in the story. The standard Greek version, attributed to the apostle John, is representative of the Bethlehem tradition. This version is found in over 200 manuscripts, but despite its obvious popularity, it is a poor representative of the original text – it is merely a summary of a much lengthier text found in Syriac manuscripts divided into six books. In the Syriac 'six-books' version, Mary goes to the tomb of Jesus daily to pray that she can leave the world and be with her Son in the heavens. On one Friday, the angel Gabriel appears to Mary and says her prayers soon will be answered. She returns to Bethlehem and prays that John and all the other apostles, some of whom have died, may attend her in her final days. In answer to her prayer, the apostles come to her on a cloud, plucked from the various locations assigned to them in the apocryphal acts.

The story seems innocuous enough so far, but it quickly takes on a disturbing anti-Jewish tone. Mary asks John for protection because 'the Jews have sworn that when my end comes they will burn my body'. To reassure her, John promises, 'your holy and precious body shall not see corruption' (10). When the Jewish priests become concerned about the healings occurring when people touch the outer wall of her room, they try to convince the governor to drive Mary out of town. Mary is spirited away to Jerusalem, but the Jewish leaders follow and try to burn down the house where she is staying. Then an angel comes to her defence and turns the fire on the malefactors. Despite obvious signs that Mary is protected by divine powers, Jewish characters stubbornly, perhaps demonically, refuse to stop their attacks, even after Mary's death. When Sunday comes, Mary's soul is taken by Jesus, and as the apostles carry Mary out on a bed, a Jew named Jephonias attacks the body. In response, an angel appears and strikes Jephonias's arms from his shoulders with a sword of fire. At the sight of the angel, the Jews finally repent, crying out that she is truly the Mother of God. As for poor Jephonias, he pleads for mercy and Peter restores his arms.

By now, the parallels with Jesus' death should be obvious to the reader: the story begins on a Friday, Mary dies on a Sunday, and she experiences opposition from Jews and resistance from a Roman governor. The parallels continue when the apostles lay Mary's body in the garden of Gethsemane in a new tomb. For three days voices of angels are heard emanating from the tomb. The voices then go silent and the apostles say, 'thereafter we all perceived that her spotless and precious body was translated into Paradise' (48).

The other version of the *Dormition*, the Palm tradition, is less well known than the Bethlehem tradition, though it appears to be the earliest, perhaps even originating in the third century. It is found today in the Ethiopian *Liber Requiei Mariae* (the *Book of Mary's Repose*), several fragmentary sources (in Syriac, Georgian and Coptic), a condensed Greek form, and a Latin version influential in the West. It also appears in Coptic homilies. Mary's death plays a much smaller part in this text. Other traditions are woven

121

into the narrative, including non-canonical stories relating to the exodus, material from the *Testament of Solomon*, and a story in which Peter and Paul fight the devil. Also found here are some aspects of Gnostic thought, including the soul's imprisonment in matter and its need to ascend after death in order to return to the heavens.

The palm of the Tree of Life enters the story at the start when Jesus appears to Mary while she is praying on the Mount of Olives. He reminds Mary of the time when the family was travelling to Egypt and the two-year-old Jesus commanded a palm tree to bend down to them so they could pluck its fruit (a story found also in the *Gospel of Pseudo-Matthew* 20). This telling of the tale includes an interesting monologue from Joseph lamenting his fate: 'And I am afflicted because I did not know the child that you have; I only know that he is not from me. But I have thought in my heart, perhaps I had intercourse with you while drunk' (6). Jesus reveals that the palm tree was expelled from Eden and then he restores it to its former home. The text goes on to narrate the story of Mary's death as in the Bethlehem tradition. The story comes to a close with Mary's body taken to paradise, where it is reunited with her soul.

The *Dormition of Mary* rarely appears in collections of Christian Apocrypha, primarily because most scholars consider it to be a relatively late text. But clearly it is important for the history of Christian doctrine about the death of Mary. The *Dormition* shows that Christians began to think about Mary's fate as early as the third century, but the doctrine of the Assumption was not finally accepted by the Catholic Church until 1950. Other churches, such as the Eastern Orthodox, also celebrate the Assumption but they do not define the teaching quite so formally. Given the influence of the *Dormition* on Christian thought about Mary, it must be ranked with the *Protevangelium of James* and the *Acts of Pilate* as the apocryphal texts that have had the greatest impact on Christian teachings.

The *History of Joseph the Carpenter*

Though Joseph was only the adoptive father of Jesus, Christian imagination nevertheless wanted to supply him also with an honourable death. The *History of Joseph the Carpenter* was composed somewhat later than the early *Dormition* traditions – perhaps in the late sixth or seventh century. It is found today only in Coptic and Arabic manuscripts. The story is framed by a dialogue between Jesus and his disciples on the Mount of Olives. The apostles ask Jesus about the death of Joseph, and what he reveals to them is written in this text.

As the aged Joseph, now 111 years old, lies on his deathbed, several details are revealed about his life. As in the *Protevangelium of James*, Joseph was chosen by lot to be the caretaker of Mary, and the brothers and sisters of Jesus are said to be children from Joseph's previous marriage. But we learn now that Jesus' stepsisters are named Lysia and Lydia, and further details are given about their mother. Joseph married at 40 and was widowed at 49. Then he spent one year alone and three with Mary before she gave birth to Jesus. This puts Joseph's death when Jesus was 18. So in *Joseph the Carpenter* we are given the only story about Jesus set in the time between his discussion with the teachers in the Temple at 12 years old and his baptism around 30 years of age by John the Baptist.

The adolescent Jesus is portrayed as quite distraught about Joseph's death. He watches his father's struggle with tears in his eyes, and tells the apostles,

> I, for my part, my beloved ones, was sitting at his head, and Mary my mother was sitting by his feet. And he lifted up his eyes to my face, but was not able to speak, for the hour of death held sway over him. He then lifted up his eyes and released a loud groan. And I held his hands and his knees for a long while, as he looked at me and beseeched me, 'Do not let me be taken away!' (19.2–5)

Jesus safeguards Joseph's soul until the angels come and deliver it to God. He then prepares Joseph's body and declares that it will not decay. Jesus promises also to reward with blessings all who properly venerate Joseph by providing an offering and depositing it in his shrine on his memorial day, as well as for good deeds done in his name, for naming a child Joseph and for copying this text. The interplay here between text and veneration is a common feature of medieval Christian Apocrypha. It demonstrates how story and practice, particularly on feast days, worked hand in hand, even for texts outside the Bible.

The *Life of John the Baptist*

Scholars of early Christianity are in universal agreement that Jesus was a follower of John the Baptist. The Gospel of Luke (1.5–80) honours this relationship by making John the cousin of Jesus and telling the story of his birth. The Gospels also narrate Jesus' baptism by John and the circumstances of John's death – he is decapitated by the Galilean king Herod Antipas because John criticized Herod for marrying the wife of his brother Philip (Mark 6.17–19 and parallels). The importance of John is reflected also in the sheer amount of references to the Baptist found in the Christian Apocrypha. In most cases John appears only in cameo or simply in a reprisal of his role from the canonical Gospels. A few little-known texts, however, expand greatly on the portrayal of John we find in the New Testament. The most important of these texts is a *Life of John the Baptist* attributed to Serapion, an Egyptian bishop of the fourth century.

The *Life of John* was composed, likely in Greek, around 385–95 CE. It survives today only in six Garshuni manuscripts of the fifteenth to eighteenth centuries. The story is told through the voice of the bishop Serapion on the occasion of an unspecified feast day for John. It begins with a harmony of details about John's birth taken from the Gospel of Luke and the *Protevangelium of James*, finishing with the death of Zechariah and Elizabeth's flight from Herod's soldiers into the desert. After five years, when John is seven years and six months old, Elizabeth dies. Jesus, 'who with his eyes sees heaven and earth' (p. 242), sees John in the desert grieving and spirits himself and Mary on a cloud to come to his aid. They bury Elizabeth and then Jesus and Mary remain another seven days to teach John how to live in the desert.

The text then shifts to John's adult career and tells the story of Herod Antipas and his affair with Philip's wife Herodias. The Gospel account is expanded with a prologue to the story of John's death, revealing that Herodias and Herod worked together to obtain Philip's land and then Herodias and her daughter left Philip to join Herod in Judaea where he 'lived daily with both of them in adultery' (p. 248). Thanks to Herodias's scheming, John is arrested and beheaded, but not before predicting the death and resurrection of Jesus and calamities that will befall Herod and

Israel. Then things get weird. Herodias wishes to defile the head of the Baptist, but to her surprise it flies up into the air and continues its criticism of Herod in the skies, first of Jerusalem and then throughout the world. After 15 years, the head lands in the town of Homs (Emesa), where it is buried by the townspeople, and a church is built upon the spot. In the meantime, Herodias, her daughter and Herod all meet grisly ends, thus allowing John's disciples to take his body (recalling Mark 6.29 / Matthew 14.12) and bury it in Sebaste, near the body of the prophet Elisha. Over time the remains are carried off to Alexandria, where Serapion, the author of the text, deposits them in a church built in the Baptist's honour.

Additional reading

The *History of Joseph the Carpenter* can be found in Ehrman–Pleše, *The Apocryphal Gospels*. Several versions of the *Dormition of Mary* are contained and/or summarized in J. K. Elliott, *The Apocryphal New Testament*, pp. 691–723, but for a much more detailed discussion of the material see Stephen J. Shoemaker, *Ancient Traditions of the Virgin Mary's Dormition and Assumption*. For the *Life of John the Baptist*, see Alphonse Mingana, 'A New Life of John the Baptist'.

The *Life of Mary Magdalene*

We finish our look at the people in Jesus' life with perhaps the most controversial figure of first-century Christianity. Mary Magdalene is featured in a number of the texts we have examined so far. She is often portrayed in apocryphal gospels asking Jesus questions in dialogue or sayings texts (the *Dialogue of the Saviour*, the *Pistis Sophia*, the *Questions of Bartholomew*), appears on occasion in the Pilate Cycle, has an entire gospel written in her name (the *Gospel of Mary*), and is mentioned in the *Gospel of Philip* as the 'companion' of Jesus. The canonical Gospels identify Mary as one of several women who 'provided for them [that is, Jesus and the Twelve Apostles] out of their resources' (Luke 8:3). It is also said that Mary had been exorcised of seven demons (Luke 8.2). Matthew, Mark and Luke place Mary among the women who witnessed the empty tomb, and in the Gospel of John she is the first person to see Jesus resurrected (John 20.1–18). According to Christian tradition, Mary Magdalene was once a repentant prostitute. There is no biblical basis for this identification, though it appears to have arisen from conflating Mary with the 'sinner' (Luke 7.37) who anoints Jesus with perfume (Mark 14.3–9 and parallels). This tendency to conflate female characters in the canonical Gospels is an identifying feature of two biographies of Mary, one that casts Mary as a saint, the other as a sinner.

The *Encomium* (or *Praise*) *of Mary Magdalene*, attributed to Cyril of Jerusalem (*c.* 313–86), is available today in two fragmentary Coptic manuscripts, but the text appears to have been translated from Greek. The text says nothing about Mary being a prostitute. Instead it calls Mary a saint and says she was a virgin from birth to her death. Mary was born to a rich noble family in Magdalia. Her father named her Mary and her mother named her Magdalene after the city of her birth. When her parents die, Mary is entrusted to the care of her older sister, Anna, the mother of the Virgin Mary according to the *Protevangelium of James*. This makes Mary Magdalene Jesus' aunt, not his wife. The text goes on to portray Mary as actively trying to prevent Jesus' execution. She writes to the emperor Tiberius, pleading for him to intervene with Herod Antipas; surprisingly, Pilate is not mentioned at all. Tiberius writes back to Mary, but Mary is unable to stop Herod's hand. Mary then instructs Nicodemus and Joseph to obtain Jesus' body for burial. As in the canonical Gospels, Mary witnesses the empty tomb, but here she fetches Jesus' mother, who instead becomes the first to see Jesus risen in the garden. Soon after, the Virgin Mary dies, and the apostles write their Gospels and head off on their preaching journeys. Mary and another disciple, Theophilus, stay in Jerusalem, where Jesus visits her and teaches her 'many hidden mysteries' (p. 204).

A far less praiseworthy portrayal of Mary is found in a Greek *Life of Mary Magdalene*, also incorporated in *The Golden Legend*. In *The Golden Legend*'s version of the story, Mary is conflated with Mary of Bethany, the sister of Martha and Lazarus (from John 11.1—12.8; Mary and Martha also appear in Luke 10.38–42). The three are born to noble parents and enjoy great riches. At their parents' death, Mary is bequeathed the walled town of Magdala, Martha is granted Bethany, and Lazarus is given a great part of

Jerusalem. Mary is tempted by her newly acquired riches, so that 'she gave her body to pleasure – so much that her proper name was forgotten and she was commonly called "the sinner"' (p. 375) – she has become Luke's sinner with the jar of perfume. After Jesus' death Mary departs with Lazarus, Martha and a few others to Marseilles. There Mary comes into contact with the prince of the province and his wife, and she is involved in their efforts to conceive a child. The story concludes with Mary departing the city and heading off into the desert for contemplation. Fed daily by angels, Mary lives there another 30 years before her death.

Mary Magdalene's portrayal as a repentant prostitute can be traced as far back as the sixth century, when Pope Gregory the Great wrote of Mary in a series of homilies. This image of Mary has endured, even despite the Vatican's better-late-than-never disavowal of the tradition in 1969. Some scholars, eager to reha-bilitate the image of Mary, draw upon apocryphal depictions of Mary to claim that she was an important early Christian leader, both before and after Jesus' death. Those who claim, without basis, that Mary was the wife of Jesus replace Mary's roles as benefactor and witness with those of romantic partner and mother. In doing so, they are just as guilty as Pope Gregory for diminishing Mary's importance in the early Church.

Sources and studies

The *Encomium of Mary Magdalene* is available only in French in René Georges Coquin and Gerard Godron, 'Un Encomium copte sur Marie-Madeleine'. The *Life of Mary Magdalene* can be read in William Granger Ryan's English translation of Voragine's *The Golden Legend* (vol. 1, pp. 364–83) or in François Halkin, 'Une Vie grecque de sainte Marie-Madeleine'. For a comprehensive treatment of canonical and apoc-ryphal Mary Magdalene traditions, see Ann Graham Brock, *Mary Magdalene, The First Apostle*.

The legends of the apostles and the stories of the family of Jesus are not considered the most exciting texts of the Christian Apocrypha. And there's good reason for that. The disarray and disorder in the texts of the apocryphal acts make the stories dif-ficult to follow, and with the constant repetition of the same themes and motifs, the texts quickly become tedious. Most of the other tales have some curious features – such as the portrayal of Judas as Oedipus, or the flying head of John the Baptist – but there is little in them that bears repeated reading. The Jesus apocrypha, by contrast, are far more appealing, with their diverse interpretations of Jesus' origins, teachings, death and resurrection. Still, we can't ignore the importance of the texts from this chapter. When written, the texts articulated Christian views and practices that came to be considered heretical, but in their edited forms they remained valuable because of what they revealed about the lives of important early Christian figures. The texts were read on feast days or in private devotion. Some even worked hand in hand with relics and cult sites to encourage proper veneration of the saint. One in particular, the *Dormition of Mary*, helped to develop and promote an important aspect of Marian devotion. So, even if the legends have less attraction to readers than the apocrypha about Jesus, they are no less important for the history of Christian life and literature.

Hopefully more people will become interested in these texts. As we have seen, several of them are still unavailable to many readers, particularly English readers. New manuscript discoveries of controversial gospels may capture the public's imagination and sell books, but scholars need to direct some of their energies also to these other texts before they become lost, this time not because of censorship by the Church, but because of scholarly neglect.

6

Myths, misconceptions and misinformation about the Christian Apocrypha

The popularity of *The Da Vinci Code* and the media coverage that attended such new discoveries as the *Gospel of Judas* have brought much attention to the Christian Apocrypha. Which is great. Scholars of these texts deserve to get more attention for their work, and I firmly believe that the texts have much to teach us about the history of Christianity and its culture. But the attention has its downside. *The Da Vinci Code* and similar popular treatments of the Christian Apocrypha are works of fiction, not scholarship; so the authors are more concerned about writing gripping thrillers than reporting the results of thorough investigation into the literature. As for the *Gospel of Judas* and other newly discovered texts, much of the discussion on these finds in the media has been obscured by loud, red-faced pundits eager to repudiate the texts by labelling them heretical or rushing to declare them forgeries. Occasionally, scholars are consulted about their opinions on apocryphal texts, but the most widely published responses have come not from experts on the Christian Apocrypha but from conservative American evangelical theologians who would prefer that all of this attention to non-canonical texts would simply go away. In the end, readers are left confused: is the New Testament an accurate representation of the life of Jesus and the history of the early Church or is it one view among many? Do the apocryphal gospels offer us the true Jesus – a merely human, proto-feminist wise man – or are the canonical Gospels correct that Jesus was the Son of God who died for our sins? *The Da Vinci Code* may have a lot of things wrong, but does this mean that traditional Christian teaching has everything right?

This final chapter looks at both sides in this dialogue: the liberal scholarship that inspired *The Da Vinci Code* and which draws heavily on the Christian Apocrypha to argue that the traditional history of early Christianity needs to be rewritten, and the responses to this scholarship from conservative theologians. It should be said at the outset that 'liberal' and 'conservative' are inadequate labels. Their use suggests that there are only two perspectives on the utility of the texts and that there is a gulf that divides them. In reality, the arguments run along a spectrum, with certain liberal scholars on one end going so far as to argue that some non-canonical texts are better representations of Jesus and the early Church than canonical texts, and certain conservatives on the other declaring that all Christian Apocrypha are late, derivative and even detrimental to a believer's faith. Between these poles lie more moderate scholars holding a variety of views on a wide array of texts.

The conservatives are perhaps better identified as 'apologists' (from Greek *apologia*, or 'speaking in defence') because their goal is to defend the New Testament as best reflecting the life of Jesus and the views of the early Church. The apologists typically come from evangelical backgrounds and teach at theological colleges. Included in their ranks are Ben Witherington, Darrell Bock, Daniel Wallace and Craig Evans, all of whom have written books aimed at refuting liberal approaches to the Christian Apocrypha. These books identify the enemies in this battle principally as Bart Ehrman, Elaine Pagels, Helmut Koester, John Dominic Crossan and Marvin Meyer, who have written both scholarly and popular works arguing for the importance of the Christian Apocrypha for reconstructing early Christian history, as well as for understanding the origins of texts in the New Testament. The liberal scholars in this conflict tend to work at secular universities or colleges; many are associated with Harvard Divinity School, or Claremont Graduate University in California, two major North American centres for the study of the Christian Apocrypha.

Unfortunately, liberals and conservatives are very poor at communicating with one another. Conservatives champion the scholarship of their like-minded colleagues and work explicitly to denigrate, and in the process often misrepresent, the results of liberal scholarship. Liberal scholars similarly seem to read only works that support their points of view; indeed, they care so little about conservative views that they ignore completely the voices of their critics. And though both groups combat for the attention of the wider public, they really only preach to the converted, with liberals appealing to an audience mistrustful of institutions and eager to challenge tradition, and conservatives writing to believers who are unlikely to be attracted to liberal scholarship anyway. This lack of communication is really too bad, because there is much that the two groups could learn from each another.

In the course of the toing and froing between the two sides (more toing than froing, really), a number of statements have been made about the non-canonical texts that are detrimental to the proper understanding and appreciation of the literature. This chapter, then, addresses the myths, misconceptions and misinformation about the Christian Apocrypha that have grown out of discussion of the texts since the publication of *The Da Vinci Code*. The aim is to bring the conversation back from the extreme ends of the spectrum to the middle, where the Christian Apocrypha are valued as expressions of the views, practices and experiences of various forms of Christianity that have existed throughout the centuries.

Sources and studies

For a look at the arguments of the apologetic writers, see Darrell L. Bock, *The Missing Gospels*; Ben Witherington, *The Gospel Code*; Darrell L. Bock and Daniel B. Wallace, *Dethroning Jesus*; and Craig Evans, *Fabricating Jesus*. The targets of their attacks include Elaine Pagels, *The Gnostic Gospels*; Bart Ehrman, *Lost Christianities*; John Dominic Crossan, *The Cross That Spoke*; Helmut Koester, *Ancient Christian Gospels*, and, in general, the work of the Jesus Seminar. For a discussion of the debate between the two groups, see Tony Burke, 'Heresy Hunting in the New Millennium'.

The Christian Apocrypha were all written after the texts of the New Testament, or the Christian Apocrypha were all written before the texts of the New Testament

In defending the authority of the New Testament, the conservative apologists argue that all the Christian Apocrypha were written after the creation of the New Testament. This comes in response to some liberal scholars who have made claims that certain non-canonical texts – chiefly the *Gospel of Thomas,* but also the *Gospel of Peter* and *Secret Mark* – were either written before the New Testament Gospels or draw upon sources used by the canonical Gospel writers. Such claims undermine the authority of the canon, because the apocryphal texts are seen as superior to canonical texts.

At the outset, it's important to remember that, before the fourth century, there was no 'New Testament'. Numerous texts circulated in the early centuries; some of these steadily gained authority as Scripture, others continued to be read over the centuries alongside Scripture, and still others were valued only by small groups of Christians and thus eventually fell into disuse. But apologists often discuss the Apocrypha in comparison with the New Testament as if the canonical texts always belonged together, as if they were composed by one person, at one time, with one voice. In reality, canonical and non-canonical texts each have their own individual history. So, when it comes to dating the texts, there are no certain answers, but it does appear that some apocryphal texts – a small number, it seems – may have been composed prior to some of those that became canonical.

We know very little about the dates of composition for the New Testament material. The authentic letters of Paul were written between 50 and 60 CE, but the Gospels and Acts, which contain few indications of their time of composition, are usually dated between 70 and 100. The remaining texts (Hebrews, Revelation, the letters of Peter, John, James, and Jude) seem to have been written after the Gospels – perhaps as late as 125. Some conservative thinkers try to date canonical texts earlier – for example, they believe Acts was written before the death of Paul, and they consider the letters of Peter to be genuine and therefore written within the apostle's lifetime – but most scholars accept the standard chronology. Still, even these dates are, at best, educated guesses. The only sure way to date ancient texts is by material evidence – that is, the manuscripts. For Christian texts, the earliest manuscript evidence comes from the second century. Papyrus 52, a scrap from the Gospel of John, is dated based on palaeographical arguments to around 125, indicating that the Gospel must have been composed before that time. But evidence as early as Papyrus 52 is quite rare; few other manuscripts have been found that date earlier than the last decades of the second century.

Another method for dating Christian texts is to look for references in the early Church writers. For example, if Justin Martyr, writing around 150, mentions a text or quotes from a text, then we know it existed before his time. But again, except for the letters of Paul, there are few clear and unequivocal references to canonical or non-canonical texts before the mid-second century. In order to date a text more narrowly, we must look at its contents, searching for some mention of historical events that occurred prior to its composition, such as the Jewish War of 66–70 CE, or the eruption of Mount Vesuvius in 79. Unfortunately, the texts include few such historical markers. We also look for indications that a text's author copied another text. For example, the Gospels of Matthew and Luke appear to have used Mark as a source (or at least the majority of scholars think so); if so, they must have been composed after Mark wrote his Gospel.

The same techniques and assumptions used to date canonical texts must be used when determining the origins of non-canonical texts. Manuscript evidence for some apocryphal gospels is surprisingly early. The fragmentary manuscripts of the *Gospel of Thomas* from Oxyrhynchus and Papyrus Egerton 2 were created at the end of the second century. The texts themselves could only have been composed decades earlier – how many decades we cannot know for certain. Consider for comparison the case of Papyrus 45, the earliest manuscript of the Gospel of Mark, dated to around 200 CE, over a century after the Jewish War when the text is believed to have been written. Perhaps a century or more also lies between the manuscripts of *Thomas* and P.Egerton 2 and the texts' composition. As for references to apocryphal texts by early Church writers, these are abundant at the end of the second century. Irenaeus (writing around 180), for example, excerpts a story from the *Infancy Gospel of Thomas*, and Clement of Alexandria (writing around 198–203) quotes several times from the *Gospel of the Egyptians*. Earlier references are harder to come by, but some of the non-canonical agrapha from *1 Clement* (dated around 95–7) and others could just as easily come from the *Gospel of Thomas* as oral tradition.

Admittedly, many apocryphal texts were composed after the canonical Gospels – the infancy gospels, for example, incorporate stories from Matthew and Luke and then add further information about Jesus' early years and his ancestry. But apocryphal texts often are altered over time, and there is a tendency in later manuscripts to harmonize with canonical texts and traditions. In many cases, the closer we come to reconstructing the original text, the fewer parallels we see with canonical material, thus weakening arguments for their dependence on canonical texts. Finally, both canonical and non-canonical texts betray evidence of having incorporated earlier sources – like Q for Matthew and Luke, or the Jewish-Christian source of the *Pseudo-Clementine Romance*. This too complicates the process of dating ancient literature. In the end, an apocryphal text can be both early and late, both dependent on the canonical Gospels and independent.

Any conclusions about dating ancient texts must be tentative, particularly when those conclusions can change with each new manuscript discovery. What is important, though, is that determinations of origins should not be tainted by a scholar's bias. There is no *a priori* reason to date apocryphal texts late and canonical texts early, or vice versa. Each text has to be evaluated separately and the evidence must be allowed to speak for itself.

The Christian Apocrypha are 'forgeries', written in the name of apostles

The modern definition of a literary forgery is a text ascribed to someone other than its true author, written with the intention to deceive. Creators of such forgeries try to imitate the writing style of the supposed author and to match the text's contents with the appropriate temporal and geographical context. In some cases they use materials for the forgery to make the copy of the text appear to come from the supposed author's time period. The use of the term 'forgery' by apologists evokes all of these elements. The Christian Apocrypha, then, are made out to be texts created to deceive their readers into accepting the lies that they contain.

Of course, the situation is more nuanced than that. Not all non-canonical or even canonical texts claim apostolic authorship. Paul's letters certainly do, and at least seven of these are widely considered to be authentic. But the Gospels and Acts seem to have been written anonymously, as was Hebrews, though tradition states that it was written by Paul. Revelation was written by someone named John, but he was not the apostle John, and the letters of John are attributed only to 'the elder' (see 2 John 1). As for apocryphal texts, many of them also lack attribution. The apocryphal acts are tales about particular apostles; they make no claims to be written by them. Similarly, some gospels, like the *Gospel of Judas* or the *Gospel of Mary*, feature prominently the characters in their titles, but are actually anonymous. Other texts, like the *Infancy Gospel of Thomas*, are attributed to early Christian figures, but the attributions were added later in the manuscript tradition. And then there are those texts named for communities which used them, not for those who wrote them, such as the *Gospel of the Hebrews*, or the *Gospel of the Egyptians*. Once we set all of these examples aside, what remains are a small number of texts, some canonical (e.g. the disputed letters of Paul, 1 and 2 Peter, perhaps James and Jude) and some non-canonical (e.g. the *Gospel of Thomas*, the *Protevangelium of James*, the *Apocalypse of Peter*) which are indeed written by someone claiming to be a Christian leader of the first century but likely were written sometime after that leader's death.

But does this make them 'forgeries'? Were they written to deceive their readers? Writing books under someone else's name, or 'pseudepigraphy', was very common in antiquity. Jews did it, Graeco-Roman polytheists did it, and Christians did it. Also common in antiquity was the belief that such a practice was wrong. When discovered, pseudepigraphical books were described venomously as 'falsely inscribed writings' and 'lies'. Faced with their cherished writings being declared fakes, conservative biblical scholars try to rescue the canonical pseudepigrapha by describing them as texts written in a 'school of thought' – that is, the author considered the ideas in the text to be that of his teacher, not his own – or the author was directed by the Holy Spirit to speak in the voice of an apostle. But neither of these explanations really works. Since virtually every writer commenting on pseudepigraphy in antiquity decried the practice, we must admit that Christian pseudepigraphers were aware that what they were doing would be condemned if they were caught. And sometimes they were caught. Remember the case of the *Acts of Paul*. Tertullian tells us that the author (or perhaps only a compiler) of the *Acts* was an elder in the church from Asia Minor who was removed from his office when it was discovered he wrote the text. And the *Acts* was not even ascribed to Paul! Really, it was condemned because of its contents, not its authorship. And that distinction is important. As mentioned in the discussion of canon selection in Chapter 1, books were accepted into the Bible more for what they contained than for who wrote them. Authorship legitimated its selection as Scripture; it did not determine it.

The *Acts of Paul* example also shows us why pseudepigraphy was practised, at least sometimes. The elder claims he created the text 'out of love for Paul'. Canonical and apocryphal pseudepigrapha were created for what the authors considered the right reasons, namely to address new developments or concerns in their communities, not, as with typical forgeries, for personal gain. Attributing their words to Paul or Peter or some other early Christian authority may not be the most honest way of dealing with issues in their communities, but it certainly would have been a more effective means of getting heard than if they wrote under their own names.

There are some examples of pseudepigraphy that are more clearly manipulative and underhanded. The *Abgar Correspondence* comes to mind. Here we have two letters, one attributed to King Abgar of Edessa, one to Jesus, composed expressly to provide evidence for the early origin of proto-orthodox Christianity in Syria. The proto-orthodox were harsh in their condemnation of other Christian groups for creating new texts, but it appears they had no qualms about doing it themselves if it was to their benefit, even going as far as to forge a letter by Jesus!

Forgeries exist both in the New Testament and among the Christian Apocrypha. If we are to disregard apocryphal texts simply because some are 'falsely ascribed', then several texts from the New Testament must be disregarded also. Keep in mind, however, that, while the majority of New Testament scholars believe certain canonical texts to be pseudonymous, a small number continue to consider them authentic. Remember too that few apocryphal texts bear attributions, and no reputable scholar of the Christian Apocrypha would ever claim that such attributions are genuine.

The Christian Apocrypha were written by Gnostics

In the late second century, Irenaeus of Lyons composed his magnum opus *On the Detection and Overthrow of Knowledge Falsely So Called* (or *Against Heresies*, for short), a catalogue of the beliefs and practices of more than a dozen Christian groups describing how each differs from 'true' (that is, proto-orthodox) Christianity. Irenaeus considered Gnostic Christianity, particularly the school of Valentinus, a dire threat to the Church. But he did not always take care to describe rival Christian groups correctly. He enjoyed accusing them of performing magic and of various immoral sexual practices (indiscriminate sex, multiple marriages, prostitution); likely, however, the accusations are false, since they seem to be a common stock of slanders that ancient writers heaped upon their enemies – even upon proto-orthodox Christianity by its critics. In identifying all of the so-called 'heretics' as Gnostics, Irenaeus continued a tradition begun by Justin Martyr of combining together all heresies and attributing their entry into 'true' Christianity to the work of one arch-heretic, identified by Irenaeus as Simon Magus. A look at Irenaeus's list of heresies – which includes the Jewish-Christian Ebionites and Syrian ascetic Encratites – demonstrates that Irenaeus is wrong to label all heresies Gnostic. But his approach is effective for focusing his attack. Gnostic Christianity becomes the boogey-man to be feared and avoided at the peril of one's soul.

The strategies of heresy hunters like Justin and Irenaeus became so engrained in Christian discourse that, until recently, scholars assumed the Christian Apocrypha were censured by the Church because they were produced by Gnostics. Scholars looked hard, though often in vain, for Gnostic elements in the texts. Today, scholars of Gnosticism are finally emerging from the shadow of the heresy hunters and working to redefine and recategorize Christian heresies based on the content of the texts they appear to have valued, not on the untrustworthy descriptions given by their proto-orthodox critics.

Despite these developments, many modern apologists continue to follow the strategy of the heresy hunters and declare that many, if not all, non-canonical Christian texts are Gnostic, a term which has accrued additional mistrust and hatred among Christians since

137

Irenaeus's day. So anything labelled 'Gnostic' becomes synonymous with malevolence, licentiousness and lies. Some apologists even cast aspersions on Christian Apocrypha scholars by calling them Gnostics, as if studying a subject automatically leads the investigator to become a follower. But this is nothing but polemical parlour tricks. Certainly some texts have ties to Gnostic thought – particularly if they contain Creation stories like the one found in the *Apocryphon of John* – but the vast majority of them, including the various infancy gospels, the Jewish-Christian gospels, and the apocryphal apocalypses, contain no Gnostic elements whatsoever. By calling the Christian Apocrypha 'Gnostic', either the apologists have not read the texts carefully, or they are not current on efforts to more carefully define Gnostic Christianity. Or maybe, like Irenaeus, they invoke Gnosticism because doing so is effective apologetic strategy.

Identifying Christian Apocrypha as Gnostic is useful for the apologists also because it allows them to date the texts later than those in the canon. No one knows the precise origins of Gnosticism. Like any religious movement, Gnosticism took centuries to develop and continues to develop even today – Gnostic groups can be found in many major cities. The assumption, however, is that Gnosticism is a mid to late second-century phenomenon. Any texts with Gnostic affinities, then, must have been composed 75 to 100 years after the New Testament texts. But the origins of Gnosticism may be more ancient than many scholars believe. Consider Simon Magus, who is portrayed as a contemporary of the apostles in the book of Acts; the heresy hunters associate his views with Gnosticism. Other Christian Gnostic thinkers – such as Saturninus and Basilides – operated in the early second century. Full-blown Gnostic texts with complex cosmogonies and distinctive roles for the Demiurge, Sophia, etc. – are definitely in circulation by the end of the second century. Irenaeus quotes extensively from the *Apocryphon of John*, for example. But we do not know how early these texts were composed.

All told, then, not all Christian Apocrypha are Gnostic, and even for those that are Gnostic, there is no guarantee that they were composed much later than the canonical texts. Keep in mind also, that some apocryphal texts, like the *Gospel of Thomas*, were altered from their original forms, with Gnostic material or

138

interpretations added to the texts over time. Clearly, dating a text based on the presence of Gnostic imagery and theology is a practice fraught with difficulties.

The Christian Apocrypha claim that Jesus was not divine

When biblical scholars study the historical Jesus, they try to keep their own religious beliefs out of their investigations. They consider Jesus a human being, not the Son of God. He ate, drank, slept and went to the bathroom just like everybody else. They assume that, over time, the Jesus story acquired more and more legendary and supernatural qualities; so any teachings or activities of Jesus that lack these qualities are more likely to be historical, or to use scholars' preferred term, authentic. Stories of Jesus' miracles, including his resurrection, are explained as either symbolic stories intended to convey a particular message (the transformation of water into wine from the Gospel of John 2.1–11, for example, demonstrates the superiority of Jesus over the wine god Dionysus; Jesus 'heals' lepers by ignoring their disease and accepting them into his band of followers) or as primitive understandings of scientifically verifiable phenomena (Jesus did not cast out demons; rather he psychoanalysed the mentally ill). So scholars of the historical Jesus are predisposed to texts that focus on teachings over miracle stories, hoping that these texts will add to our knowledge of what Jesus said and help us understand as a result how he gained a following.

Several apocryphal texts contain sayings of Jesus that are not found in the canonical Gospels. The *Gospel of Thomas*, for example, contains 114 separate sayings of Jesus, some without parallel in the New Testament. Could these be authentic sayings of Jesus? *Thomas* also contains very little narrative – there is no birth story, no crucifixion and no resurrection. Some scholars take from this that *Thomas* is a witness to a form of Christianity that did not put theological value in Jesus' birth and death; salvation comes not from Jesus' self-sacrifice on the cross but from the proper interpretation of his teachings. Could this form of Christianity be more true to the original message and mission of Jesus? Other texts that contain sayings of Jesus – such as the *Gospel of Philip* and dialogue texts like the *Apocryphon of James* – also receive much attention from historical Jesus scholars. The young miracle-worker of the *Infancy Gospel of Thomas* or the ghostly guide of the *Apocalypse of Peter* are too distant from the human Jesus to be of much use.

Apologists are quick to point out that even the *Gospel of Thomas* contains some indications that the text's author considered Jesus to be much more than human. In one saying, Jesus seems to speak of his divinity when he declares, 'It is I who am the light upon them all. It is I who am the all. It is from me that the all has come, and to me that the all has extended' (log. 77). He suggests also that, though divine, he came into the world and 'appeared . . . in the flesh' (log. 28). The apologists criticize liberal scholars for arguing that the *Gospel of Thomas* is a better witness to Jesus than the New Testament texts because *Thomas* presents Jesus as human. In response, the apologists contend that the Jesus of the *Gospel of Thomas* is more divine, more supernatural, not less.

To be fair, however, none of the liberal scholars actually claim that *Thomas*'s Jesus is merely human. Their argument is only that sayings are better than narratives for reconstructing the historical Jesus. Texts that prominently feature sayings, whether canonical or non-canonical, will be useful for this purpose. And despite the protestations of the apologists, most scholars would agree with this premise. Even some of the apologists concede that a small portion of the unique sayings from *Thomas* may have been spoken by Jesus. Putting *Thomas* aside, it's worth mentioning that there are, indeed, a few apocryphal texts that portray Jesus as human. Jewish Christians considered Jesus a normal human being, not a Son of God. So their texts feature no accounts of the virgin birth. Instead Jesus is presented like a prophet, and in this capacity he is able to work miracles, just as Elijah and Elisha did before him. Oddly enough, the apologists don't mention these texts in their arguments against liberal scholars, likely because studies of the Jewish-Christian apocrypha have made far less impact on non-scholarly readers than work on the *Gospel of Thomas*.

All Christian texts – canonical and non-canonical, Gnostic and non-Gnostic, Jewish or Gentile – develop the story of Jesus in their own unique ways. All of them are interpretations, though certainly some stray further from Jesus' first-century Jewish context than others. The historical Jesus scholars are on methodologically solid ground by focusing on sayings material, which tends to remain stable over time, over narrative, which tends to be more fluid. And those who incorporate the Christian Apocrypha into their investigations rightly ignore the distinction between canonical and non-canonical texts, a distinction important for Christians but not for scholars, whose goal should be to piece together history using all available sources. The apologists, on the other hand, while correct to point out that apocryphal texts interpret, transform and elaborate the Jesus traditions, must concede that so, too, do the texts of the New Testament.

The Christian Apocrypha are bizarre and fanciful compared to the canonical Gospels

As part of their efforts to demonstrate that the Christian Apocrypha do not present Jesus as 'merely human', the apologists present their readers with examples from apocryphal texts of some pretty bizarre stuff, such as the talking cross of the *Gospel of Peter*, or the cursing stories of the *Infancy Gospel of Thomas*. The canonical Gospels, in comparison, are said to be much more sober in their presentations of Jesus and, by implication, more historically valid. When discussing the Christian Apocrypha it is very tempting to focus on their more outlandish elements; and I can be accused of doing the same in this book. But it should be made clear that non-canonical texts often incorporate material from canonical texts; so there is much in them that is 'orthodox'. Furthermore, the apologists need to look more closely at the New Testament texts because they too have some peculiar features. The last time I checked, virgin births, walking on water, stilling storms, multiplying loaves and fishes, and rising from the grave were not common occurrences. The Gospel of Luke contains other odd stories. When an angry mob tried to hurl Jesus off a cliff, he mysteriously 'passed through the midst of them and went on his way' (4.30). On the Mount of Olives before his arrest, Jesus was in such anguish that his sweat was like 'great drops of blood' (22.43–44). Compared to these stories, is a talking cross really that strange? As for curse stories like those in *Infancy Thomas*, the book of Acts also contains curses – God strikes down Ananias and Sapphira (5.1–6) and King Herod (12.20–23), and blinds Paul; and Paul blinds the false prophet Elymas (13.4–12). How are these any different from the curses of the young Jesus?

True, non-canonical texts tend to include more outlandish material than the canonical texts – the apocryphal acts often feature talking animals, and the *Life of John the Baptist* has a flying, talking head – but the difference is only one of degree. It is not fair to call the Christian Apocrypha bizarre and not accede that the New Testament texts also contain fantastic elements. Fantastic, of course, to us, but not so bizarre to ancient readers, who would find all of these texts consistent with how they understood the interplay of the divine and human in their world. Ancient texts should not be judged by modern standards, nor should our familiarity with the New Testament obscure the fact that the canonical texts are pretty strange at times too.

The Christian Apocrypha were written to undermine or replace the canonical texts

The modern apologists often state that one cannot read non-canonical texts alongside canonical texts. In antiquity and today, the two categories of literature are irreconcilable. Darrell Bock addresses the issue when he states,

> These texts, on each side of the debate, force a choice. Either the Gnostic texts reflect what Jesus was and is, or the four Gospels are the best witnesses to the movement that Jesus generated. One cannot have it both ways.   (*Breaking the Da Vinci Code*, p. 89)

In some cases, Bock is correct. Some apocryphal texts were clearly written to contest proto-orthodox Christian doctrine, which is reflected in and has grown out of the texts of the New Testament. Most often, however, the Christian Apocrypha are not incompatible with canonical texts, and evidence shows that some early Christian heretical groups valued the same texts as proto-orthodox Christians.

Very early on, the four canonical Gospels and the letters of Paul seem to have acquired widespread authority. Even Tatian, known for his combination of the four Gospels into the harmony known as the *Diatessaron*, clearly valued the canonical Gospels, though he had no problem transforming them for his needs. And writers of apocryphal texts routinely incorporated canonical Gospel traditions. The *Protevangelium of James*, for example, harmonizes and expands the infancy narratives of Luke and Matthew, the *Acts of*

Pilate combines material from all four canonical Passion Narratives, and the apocryphal letters of Paul (*3 Corinthians* and *Laodiceans*) mostly repeat what Paul says in the canonical letters. This deference to New Testament traditions continues in more recent Christian Apocrypha – that is, texts composed after the formation of the 27-book Western canon in the fourth century. None of these texts explicitly contradict what is in the New Testament. As we discussed back in Chapter 2, medieval Christians seemed to care little about the boundary between canonical and non-canonical literature. Certainly for them, texts from both categories could be read together.

The case is different, however, for texts that explicitly argue against proto-orthodox doctrine. The *Revelation of Peter*, for example, challenges the view that Jesus died on the cross, and criticizes proto-orthodox bishops and deacons for believing 'they received authority from god'; instead, they are 'dry canals' (79.25–31). Similarly, the *Acts of John* re-imagines portions of the canonical Gospels, claiming again that Jesus was not truly crucified. Jesus himself says in the text, 'I was reckoned to be what I am not, not being what I was to many others; but they will call me something else, which is vile and not worthy of me' (99). And then there's the *Gospel of Judas*, which declares that the apostles, representing proto-orthodoxy, worship a false god, and accuses them of the kinds of slanders the heresy hunters levelled against Gnostics: 'some have sex with men. Some perform acts of [murder]. Some commit all sorts of sins and lawless deeds. And the men who stand [before] the altar call upon your (i.e. Jesus') [name]' (38.20–26). Few other texts actively seem intent on undermining traditions in the canonical Gospels, and even those mentioned here incorporate some of the traditions common to all Christians.

We know too that heretical Christian groups valued some of the canonical texts, though they interpreted them differently from the proto-orthodox. The New Testament Gospels are ambiguous in places and lend themselves to multiple interpretations. The Gospel of Mark, for example, begins not with a story of Jesus' birth but with Jesus' baptism. Some early Christians who did not agree with the teaching of the virgin birth would find Mark's Gospel congenial to their beliefs. Similarly, Gnostic Christians who considered Jesus a divine being sent to earth by the powers of light could agree with much of John's Gospel. We know also from Irenaeus that some heretical groups, like the followers of Valentinus, participated in worship with other Christians, but met separately for more sophisticated discussions. The Valentinians, then, presumably considered authoritative the texts popular among all Christians (the four canonical Gospels and Paul's letters) but privately composed and read texts of their own creation. So, for all the apologists' claims to the contrary, early Christians did read both canonical and non-canonical texts; and modern Christians should be able to do the same.

The Christian Apocrypha were enormously popular before their suppression by a powerful minority in the Church

According to Leigh Teabing, the Grail scholar from *The Da Vinci Code*, more than 80 gospels were in circulation before the formation of the canon, and these were excluded from the Bible because the emperor Constantine wanted to portray Jesus as divine, not human. Well, we have already seen that few texts of the Christian Apocrypha say that Jesus was merely human, and we know that the canonical Gospels likely were composed in the first century, not the fourth. The Gospels' popularity among proto-orthodox and heretical groups also demonstrates that they were hardly the views of only a 'minority'. The emergence of the New Testament is a reflection of how popular the texts within it had become; they represent a consensus among Christians about the beliefs that became widespread. The consensus emerged at least in part because the texts championed by the Roman Church were more universalistic; they were easier to understand and did not advocate asceticism, a lifestyle that fewer and fewer Christians were willing to adopt.

Some Christian groups suffered with the formation of the New Testament canon. Jewish Christians and Gnostic groups like the Manichaeans and Marcionites went underground or completely ceased to exist. But these are actions of a powerful majority imposing their will on a minority, not the reverse.

Keep in mind also that popularity is relative. As noted in Chapter 2, the available manuscript evidence of Christian literature from the first few centuries is balanced between canonical and non-canonical texts. It may be a stretch to use this evidence to suggest that the two groups of texts enjoyed equal esteem and reader-ship, but these are tantalizing possibilities. Manuscript evidence also indicates that, in medieval times, several apocryphal texts were enormously popular. Hundreds of manuscripts survive of the *Protevangelium of James*, the *Gospel of Pseudo-Matthew* and the *Gospel of Nicodemus*, and martyrdoms cut from the apocryphal acts also were widely copied and read. Often orthodox copyists would eliminate material from apocryphal texts they found offensive, but they continued to be copied and read despite commands to avoid or destroy them.

The Christian Apocrypha are being used to rewrite Christian history

Recent discussion of the Christian Apocrypha has included a re-examination of the so-called Bauer Thesis. Discussed in Chapter 1, this thesis is based on the work of Walter Bauer who sought to argue, against Church tradition, that in some parts of the ancient world, heretical forms of Christianity were established before orthodoxy. Growing out of the thesis is a relativistic view of early Christianity – that is, no one form of Christianity has more of a claim to truth than another; one group's 'orthodoxy' is another group's 'heresy'. This viewpoint is troublesome to the apologists because, once again, it undermines the authority of Christian Scripture. If orthodox Christianity as reflected in the New Testament is not the one and only true form of Christianity, they might ask, then why follow it at all?

After Bauer wrote his book, new discoveries like the Nag Hammadi Library changed much of the data Bauer used to formulate his thesis. For many of the major centres discussed in the book – Rome, Antioch, Egypt, Asia Minor – it seemed that Bauer was wrong; only in Edessa, where proto-orthodoxy did not gain strength until at least the third century, was the Bauer Thesis still persuasive. Nevertheless, a number of liberal scholars continue to champion the thesis, much to the apologists' surprise. That's because, despite his failures, Bauer rightly called into question the traditional history of the Church, which maintains that Christianity began with fundamental agreement among Jesus' followers, that orthodoxy was established very early after Jesus' death, and that heretical forms of Christianity resulted from outside corrupting influences, such as the Gnostic interest in Platonic theory. I say 'rightly' because traditions need to be challenged, even if the investigation proves tradition correct. As it turns out, many scholars believe the traditional history is wrong. Christianity seems to have grown somewhat haphazardly in the first few centuries, with multiple forms of the faith operating around the Mediterranean world. Only later did some of these groups come together in agreement to form orthodoxy.

This realization does not mean that the New Testament texts, many of which are indeed very old, are not still historically valuable; it simply means that they represent one of many varieties of Christianity, each equal in the sense that they all deserve to be studied. It may well be that the New Testament texts represent the life and teachings of Jesus better than non-canonical texts, but we will never know that for sure. All told, scholars are indeed using the Christian Apocrypha to rewrite Christian history, but I'd like to think that, in the process, they are writing better history.

Reading the Christian Apocrypha is harmful to one's faith

The ancient heresy hunters wrote their refutations because they worried about the possibility that orthodox Christians would be attracted to heretical ideas and the texts that contained them. They were trying to build a cohesive community, with a shared faith and a system of beliefs that was accessible to everyone. Modern apologists are no different. They worry too that their community will be fractured, but their concern is less that Christians will become enamoured with heresies (after all, few heretical Christian groups exist today) and more that knowledge of the Christian Apocrypha will fill them with such doubt that they will abandon the faith altogether. But is such knowledge really harmful to the reader's faith? The answer is yes. And no.

In my years as a biblical studies professor I have seen many students experience crises of faith. These students, raised in conservative Christian communities, came into my courses having never been exposed to historical-critical approaches to the Bible. They never questioned the authorship of the Gospels, or the historical veracity of traditions about Jesus, and few knew anything about the Christian Apocrypha. To them, the Bible was a historical document, written by the apostles and assembled under the guidance of the Holy Spirit. And that was that. But a few weeks into class, they found themselves convinced by scholarly arguments that called into question everything they had been brought up to believe. They felt cheated, misled, manipulated.

My own introduction to biblical scholarship was very similar. I grew up in England in a Roman Catholic home, though my family was not particularly devout. My father was greatly interested in religious questions – Who was Jesus? What happens when we die? Did Marian apparitions truly occur? When will the apocalypse happen? – but not overly concerned with religious practice; indeed, we rarely attended church. But I did believe. I believed the Gospels were written by the apostles of Jesus, I believed I had to be good if I wanted to avoid eternal damnation, and I worried intensely about signs of the end time indicated by the escalation of Cold War tensions.

These beliefs stayed with me into my years at university in Canada. My curiosity and anxiety about religious questions led me to select a major, along with English literature, in religious studies. My first religion course was a study of Jewish apocalyptic literature. I was surprised to learn that there were ancient Jewish texts similar in genre to the book of Daniel – such as *1 Enoch*, *2 Baruch* and the *Testaments of the Twelve Patriarchs* – that were not included in the Bible. That single course changed my entire perspective on the Bible. I saw how the troubling imagery and dire warnings of the Christian book of Revelation were a first-century development of literary and theological motifs found in the earlier apocalyptic texts; they were not the product of an ecstatic vision of the future, but elements in a carefully composed and finely crafted example of a genre of literature completely understandable to ancient audiences but somewhat mysterious to modern Christians. Reading these texts in their original contexts tamed the horror of them for me. I learned then that even a small amount of biblical literacy could go a long way towards reducing the anxiety brought on by my Catholic upbringing. What a revelation!

So began my fascination with the academic study of the Bible and with non-canonical literature in particular. My eyes were opened but, at the same time, I felt that I had been deceived. Why hadn't anyone ever mentioned these ideas to me before? In all my years of religious instruction in Catholic schools, how come no one ever said that there was doubt about the apostolic author-ship of the Gospels? Or that Paul likely did not write some of the letters in his name? Or that other gospels existed, with portrayals of Jesus that were very different from those found in the Bible?

But not everyone reacts this way. Students from Christian communities that are more open to discussing the results of scholarly inquiry feel little anxiety in biblical studies classrooms. Their beliefs and experience of Jesus are less tangled in texts and tradition and more connected to Jesus the man. The New Testament Gospels are seen as early attempts to understand Jesus and record his career, but, as human efforts to embrace the divine, they are inherently flawed. From this perspective, non-canonical gospels can be considered sympathetically as additional interpretations of Jesus, though perhaps more distant from their subject in time and place than the canonical texts. And this last point is an important one: remaining Christian must involve making a decision about which texts are most valuable for establishing who Jesus was. Relativism and faith cannot co-exist – a scholar can study all forms of Christianity with equal consideration and without making a judgement, but a believer cannot practise all forms of Christianity at once.

I often caution students also that biblical studies courses do not offer truth, just a perspective – the scholarly perspective. And biblical scholarship, though it seeks valiantly to understand the texts as they were written (by establishing the original context of the author and the audience) and how they were written (by considering the sources used and how they were transformed by the author), is not perfect. Our knowledge of the ancient world is fragmentary, and new information, new texts and new insights constantly affect our approaches to the literature. So there are no firm conclusions in scholarship. And when it comes to the Christian Apocrypha, the theories offered by scholars, whether radical or moderate, about how the texts impact our knowledge of the Bible or of Christian history should not worry readers, because, in the end, they are only theories.

The apologists are correct that modern Christians, to remain Christians, must make a choice about the texts they read, but it need not mean choosing the canonical texts over the non-canonical, or vice versa. Given that Jesus said and did far more than what is recorded in the New Testament, and that even some of the traditions recorded in official Scripture may not be authentic, there seems to me to be little harm in reading apocryphal texts for insight about Jesus. To some extent, the origins of the texts are immaterial. Whether a text is canonical or non-canonical, early or late, anonymous or pseudonymous, fact or fiction, it offers readers a window into how other people have sought understanding about their place in the world. And we can learn from their experiences. Wisdom, they say, can be found in strange places, even in Christian Apocrypha.

7

Parting words

So this is the end. This all-too-brief study of the Christian Apocrypha is finished. But there is still so much more that remains to be said about these texts. The surveys in Chapters 3 to 5 cover all of the best-documented apocryphal texts – including infancy gospels, Jewish-Christian gospels, Gnostic dialogues, acts and apocalypses – and a number of lesser-known texts, but more still deserve mention, such as the *Dialogue of the Paralytic with Christ*, *On the Priesthood of Jesus*, the *Letter of Christ from Heaven*, the *Beheading of John the Baptist*, the *Lament of the Virgin*, and more. Then there's the Jewish Pseudepigrapha written by Christians; modern Christian Apocrypha, such as the *Unknown Life of Christ* and the *Archko Volume*; and apocryphal texts written by non-Christians, such as the Muslim *Gospel of Barnabas* and the Jewish *Toldedoth Yeshu*. So, if your hunger for the Christian Apocrypha is unsatisfied, then don't stop here. Read the complete texts and look deeper into the scholarship. *Secret Scriptures Revealed* is merely an appetizer; the main course awaits.

But before we part, let me leave you with a few final thoughts. For many people, both scholars and casual readers, the Christian Apocrypha are interesting because they may, just may, contain secrets about Jesus and early Christianity that the Church would prefer to stay hidden. Such mistrust of institutions is part of western culture these days, and given the history of ecclesiastical corruption and misconduct, not unwarranted. This is a time also when many people are sensitive to issues of censorship. Thanks to the internet, freedom of information has never been more valued or attainable, and restrictions on the exchange of knowledge are met with stiff resistance. So it stands to reason that there must be *something* in the Christian Apocrypha that is dangerous to the Church. Why else would they try to destroy them? But how likely is it that the Christian Apocrypha actually reveal 'truths' concealed from the public for almost 2,000 years?

As it happens, the only 'truth' to be found in these texts is that Christian writers sure had vivid imaginations. They did their thinking through story, taking characters near and dear to their fellow Christians and casting them in tales in which their speech and actions offer guidance for readers living in the writers' own time. Little of the material from the stories is likely to have originated with Jesus and his contemporaries, though it is not impossible. In my thinking, it doesn't really matter. The value of the texts, as often stated in the preceding pages, is in what they tell us about Christianity, not Christ. Each story, each saying, discloses something about the writer and the community in which he or she belonged – their beliefs, their practices and their responses to the world around them. That is what these secret scriptures reveal.

Another important lesson to take from this book is the complex relationship between canonical and non-canonical literature. It is often believed that, with the formation of the New Testament in the fourth century, apocryphal texts went underground, surfacing only when discovered in musty old libraries or archaeological sites. But, as we have seen, Christians throughout the centuries continued to be exposed to apocryphal traditions, whether through the texts themselves (since many of them continued to circulate), or through homilies, art and drama. We know, too, that the distinction between what is canonical and non-canonical is not always clear – the canon varies over time and place, and sometimes non-canonical material enters canonical tradition (such as the addition of the Woman Caught in Adultery in the Gospel of John, or the inclusion of the *Epistle to the Laodiceans* in some biblical manuscripts). Arguably, the separation of canonical and non-canonical texts became clear only with the creation of the printing press, which made copies of the Bible widely available. But the printing press also helped to disperse apocryphal texts, at first for devotional reading and later for the service of scholars who, in their search for the texts' origins, reignited conflicts over the significance of the Christian Apocrypha, conflicts that continue today. As long as the Christian Apocrypha are considered a secondary body of literature, useful at times but nevertheless inferior to the Bible, theologians and Church officials seem willing to leave well enough alone. But suggest that apocryphal texts are earlier or superior to the canonical and the détente collapses.

However, all is not grim for the Christian Apocrypha today. The texts receive more attention now than they have received in decades. The texts and traditions appear regularly in popular culture – including Dan Brown's *The Da Vinci Code* and other 'secret scrolls' novels; films like *Stigmata* from 1999, which draws heavily on the *Gospel of Thomas*; and music, like Tori Amos's 'Original Sinsuality', which uses imagery from the *Apocryphon of John*. And numerous documentaries have been produced in the past ten years – such as *Banned from the Bible* (2003 and 2007) and *Secret Lives of Jesus* (2006) – to meet the public's interest in the texts. There is no end, also, to the creation of apocryphal texts, whether as forgeries made to look like ancient texts or as the reports of visionaries claiming to offer new teachings of Jesus for a new age. The Christian Apocrypha will always have their critics, but it's clear that both canonical and non-canonical texts will continue their centuries-long interplay in Christian culture. And I think we are all the better for it.

Appendix
Resources for further
study of the Christian Apocrypha

The Christian Apocrypha is a growing field of study, particularly because so many scholars have come to realize that the texts are vital for understanding early Christianity. But medievalists also see their value, and interest has been shown recently in modern apocrypha – texts written in the past few centuries, though their publishers claimed they were lost texts from antiquity. It is an international field, observable particularly in scholars' contributions to comprehensive anthologies of texts in a range of modern languages and in several series of critical editions.

English readers' best resources for the primary texts are the two collections of J. K. Elliott's *The Apocryphal New Testament* (1993; reprinted in 2005) and *The Apocryphal Gospels* by Bart Ehrman and Zlatko Pleše (2010). Elliott's edition is an update of an earlier collection by M. R. James published in 1924 and reprinted with corrections in 1953. James's collection is available in many libraries, and some of his translations of the texts appear online, but these are now quite out of date. Elliott's update includes a wide range of texts – gospels, acts, letters and apocalypses – and each text is accompanied by an extensive bibliography; these bibliographies are excellent starting points for further research. Elliott has also written a lively introduction to the literature, entitled *The Apocryphal Jesus: Legends of the Early Church* (1996), and a useful resource for the study of infancy gospels, called *A Synopsis of the Apocryphal Nativity and Infancy Narratives* (2006). The Ehrman–Pleše collection focuses only on apocryphal gospels, but contains additional texts not included by Elliott. The texts featured appear in their original languages (Greek, Latin and Coptic) as well as in English translation. Helpful also is Ehrman's other compilation, *Lost Scriptures* (2003), a companion to his book *Lost Christianities* and similar in breadth to Elliott, though covering the texts in less depth. For new text-critical work, look to the Oxford Early Christian Gospel Texts series headed by Christopher Tuckett and Andrew Gregory. To date, only two books have appeared in the series – *The Gospel of Mary* (by Tuckett, 2007) and *Gospel Fragments* (by Kraus, Kruger and Nicklas, 2008) – but volumes are planned on the Jewish-Christian gospels, the *Gospel of Judas* and the *Epistle to the Apostles*.

In North America, Polebridge Press, the publishing wing of the controversial Jesus Seminar, has published five volumes of translations in their Early Christian Apocrypha series: the *Acts of Thomas*, the *Acts of Paul*, the *Acts of Peter*, the *Acts of Andrew* and the *Epistle to the Apostles*. The group is responsible also for *The Complete Gospels*, an entry reader's collection of canonical and non-canonical gospels, edited by Robert J. Miller (fourth edition, 2010), as well as a critical edition of the *Gospel of the Savior* (by Charles Hedrick and Paul Mirecki, 1999), and a Greek and English edition of *The Infancy Gospels of James and Thomas* (by Ronald Hock, 1996). The Jesus Seminar's interest is in early texts, particularly those that may have some bearing on the life and teachings of the historical Jesus. For later texts, readers can turn to the multi-volume collection of little-known and newly published texts in translation entitled *New Testament Apocrypha: More Non-canonical Scriptures*, edited by Tony Burke and Brent Landau. The first volume in the series is due in 2014 and will feature the *Life of John the Baptist by Serapion*, the *Encomium of Mary Magdalene*, and many others.

German scholars have contributed significantly to the study of the texts; their impact is felt in a series of indispensable Christian Apocrypha collections. The first of these, Edgar Hennecke's *Neutestamentliche Apokryphen in deutscher Übersetzung*, appeared in 1904 along with a more detailed companion *Handbuch*. A second edition in 1924 revised both volumes into one. But it was the two-volume 1959/64 revision made with Wilhelm Schneemelcher that was more influential, as it was the first to be translated into English. This revision and a second translation of the fifth German edition in 1987/9 edited solely by Schneemelcher became important resources for English scholars, unsurpassed even by Elliott's edition. Nevertheless, the Hennecke–Schneemelcher collections have been criticized by some scholars for being too narrowly focused. Like the Elliott volume they favour early texts (first to fourth centuries) and texts generically similar to those found in the New Testament (gospels, acts, letters and apocalypses), leaving many other texts unexamined. Taking heed of this criticism, the new edition (the first volume of which appeared in 2012), entitled *Antike christliche Apokryphen in deutscher Übersetzung* and this time edited by Christoph Markschies and Jens Schröter, includes new and formerly unpublished texts composed as late as the eighth century.

The first significant Christian Apocrypha collection in French was the 1856 *Dictionnaire des Apocryphes* edited by Jacques-Paul Migne, a scholar best known for his collections of patristic texts, the *Patrologia graeca* and the *Patrologia latina*. The *Dictionnaire* was followed by the more focused *Évangiles apocryphes* by Charles Michel and Paul Peeters in 1911/14. Almost a century elapsed before the publication of another collection. This was assembled by the Association pour l'étude de la littérature apocryphe chrétienne (l'AELAC), formed in 1981 by a group of French and Swiss scholars with the express purpose of creating a collection of Christian Apocrypha in French translation. But their mandate quickly grew. The scholars of the group also publish highly regarded critical editions and concordances in their Corpus Christianorum Series Apocryphorum, contribute articles to the annual journal *Apocrypha*, and write pocketbook editions of individual texts (in La collection de poche Apocryphes). Their French collection, the two-volume *Écrits apocryphes chrétiens*, edited by François Bovon, Jean-Daniel Kaestli and Pierre Geoltrain, finally appeared in 1997 and 2005. It is an invaluable resource, with up-to-date introductions and translations based on new text-critical work. Though the collection and the pocketbooks cater to French audiences, l'AELAC's other publishing endeavours – Corpus Christianorum Series Apocryphorum and *Apocrypha* – feature work in a variety of languages, reflecting the increasingly international character of the group.

Other collections have appeared in Spanish, Italian, Dutch, Polish, Afrikaans, Norwegian and Czech. Of these the most significant are the Italian anthologies by Luigi Moraldi (*Apocrifi del Nuovo Testamento*, 1971, with a second edition in 1994) and Mario Erbetta (*Gli apocrifi del Nuovo Testamento*, 1975–81). Like the new German and French collections, these contain a wide assortment of texts along with detailed introductions.

Additional resources for English readers include a comprehensive bibliography of *The New Testament Apocrypha and Pseudepigrapha* by James Charlesworth. Published in 1987, the bibliography is now out of date, but is valuable for examining older scholarship. Also useful is Charlesworth's article, 'Research on the New Testament Apocrypha and Pseudepigrapha' (1988), which includes a condensed bibliography, a brief overview of phases in scholarship, and a discussion of pressing issues in the study of the literature. The best recent, and concise, introduction to the Christian Apocrypha are the two volumes prepared by Hans-Josef Klauck, one for apocryphal gospels (2002) and one for apocryphal acts (2005); these were written in German but are also available in English translation. Even more concise is Paul Foster's *The Apocryphal Gospels: A Very Short Introduction* (2009).

The internet has yet to be exploited as a fruitful medium for promoting and advancing scholarship on the Christian Apocrypha. Print publishing remains the favoured avenue for text-critical work and bibliographical resources, despite the obvious benefits presented by electronic media. But some online resources are available. Old scholarship in the public domain is accessible via sites like 'Internet Archive', and century-old translations of texts appear in such locations as Peter Kirby's 'Early Christian Writings', 'New Advent', and the 'Noncanonical Literature' page administered by the Wesley Center for Applied Theology in Idaho, USA. Several scholars have created sites based on their own particular interests – for example, Andrew Bernhard's 'gospels.net' on gospel fragments, Stephen Shoemaker's collection of 'Early Traditions of the Virgin Mary's Dormition', and my own pages dedicated to the *Infancy Gospel of Thomas* and 'More Christian Apocrypha'. Unfortunately, given the demands placed on many scholars' time, these sites tend to be neglected.

The most dynamic venue on the internet for news and discussions of apocryphal texts is the scholarly weblogs. The first of these to be launched, to my knowledge, was my own blog 'Apocryphicity', which debuted in 2006. It was followed shortly after by April DeConick's 'The Forbidden Gospels', which focuses on Gnostic texts, and then Timo Panaanen's 'Salainen evankelista', dedicated to the *Secret Gospel of Mark*. The most recent addition to the Christian Apocrypha blogosphere is Alin Suciu's self-titled blog where he offers previews of his work reassembling the manuscripts from the White Monastery. A few other blogs discuss apocryphal texts on occasion (Mark Goodacre's 'NT Blog' and Jim Davila's 'PaleoJudaica' are notable).

The internet is used also by academic societies for the dissemination of news on conferences and publications. The AELAC site is a goldmine of resources, including announcements of the annual meetings in Dole, details on the group's publishing projects, bibliographies of recent scholarship, and its membership contact list. The web page of the Westar Institute, home to the Jesus Seminar, provides information on their publishing efforts (including Christian Apocrypha-related works) and access to select articles from their journal *The Fourth R*.

Additional reading

Details for all the print resources mentioned above are provided in the bibliography. URLs for the web-based resources are not provided as sites often change location. To find the resource, simply enter both the name of the site and its administrator (if provided) into a search engine.

Bibliography

Bauckham, Richard, James R. Davila and Alexander Panayotov, eds. *Old Testament Pseudepigrapha: More Noncanonical Scriptures.* Grand Rapids, MI: Eerdmans, 2013.

Bauer, Walter. *Orthodoxy and Heresy in Earliest Christianity.* Trans. Philadelphia Seminar on Christian Origins. Philadelphia: Fortress, 1971. Translation of *Rechtgläubigkeit und Ketzerei im ältesten Christentum.* 2nd edn, Tübingen: Mohr (Siebeck), 1964. 1st edn, 1934.

Baum, Paull Franklin. 'The Mediaeval Legend of Judas Iscariot.' *PMLA* 31.3 (1916): 481–632.

Bentley, James. *Secrets of Mount Sinai: The Story of the World's Oldest Bible – Codex Sinaiticus.* Garden City, NY: Doubleday, 1986.

Bock, Darrell L. *The Missing Gospels: Unearthing the Truth behind Alternative Christianities.* Nashville: Thomas Nelson, 2006.

———. *Breaking the Da Vinci Code: Answers to the Questions Everyone's Asking.* Nashville: Thomas Nelson, 2004.

Bock, Darrell L. and Daniel B. Wallace. *Dethroning Jesus: Exposing Popular Culture's Quest to Unseat the Biblical Christ.* Nashville: Thomas Nelson, 2007.

Bovon, François. 'Editing the Apocryphal Acts of the Apostles.' Pages 1–35 in *The Apocryphal Acts of the Apostles.* Edited by François Bovon et al. Cambridge, MA: Harvard University Press, 1999.

Bovon, François, Pierre Geoltrain and Jean-Daniel Kaestli, eds. *Écrits apocryphes chrétiens.* 2 vols. Bibliothèque de la Pléiade 442 and 516. Paris: Gallimard, 1997/2005.

Brock, Ann Graham. *Mary Magdalene, The First Apostle: The Struggle for Authority.* Harvard Theological Studies 51. Cambridge, MA: Harvard University Press, 2003.

Brown, Dan. *The Da Vinci Code.* New York: Doubleday, 2004.

Budge, Ernest A. W. *Coptic Apocrypha in the Dialect of Upper Egypt.* Oxford: Longman and Co., 1913.

———. *The History of the Blessed Virgin Mary and the History of the Likeness of Christ.* 2 vols. London: Luzac & Co., 1899.

Burke, Tony, ed. *Ancient Gospel or Modern Forgery? The Secret Gospel of Mark in Debate.* Eugene, OR: Cascade, 2012.

———. 'Heresy Hunting in the New Millennium.' *Studies in Religion/Sciences Religieuses* 39 (2010): 405–20.

Burrus, Virginia. *Chastity as Autonomy: Women in the Stories of the Apocryphal Acts.* Studies in Women and Religion 23. Lewiston, NY: Edwin Mellen, 1987.

Cartlidge, David R. and J. Keith Elliott. *Art and the Christian Apocrypha.* London and New York: Routledge, 2001.

Charlesworth, James H. 'Research on the New Testament Apocrypha and Pseudepigrapha.' *ANRW* 25.2: 3919–68. Part 2, *Principat,* 25.2. Edited by H. Temporini and W. Haase. New York: De Gruyter, 1988.

———. *The New Testament Apocrypha and Pseudepigrapha: A Guide to Publications, with Excurses on Apocalypses.* Chicago: American Theological Library Association, 1987.

———, ed. *Old Testament Pseudepigrapha.* 2 vols. London: Darton, Longman & Todd, 1984.

Coquin, René Georges and Gerard Godron. 'Un Encomium copte sur Marie-Madeleine attribué à Cyrille de Jérusalem.' *Bulletin de l'Institut français d'archéologie orientale* 90 (1990): 169–212.

Court, John M. *The Book of Revelation and the Johannine Apocalyptic Tradition.* Journal for the Study of the New Testament Supplement Series 190. Sheffield: Sheffield Academic Press, 2000.

Crossan, John Dominic. *The Cross That Spoke: The Origins of the Passion Narrative.* San Francisco: Harper & Row, 1988.

Davies, Stevan L. *The Revolt of the Widows: The Social World of the Apocryphal Acts.* Carbondale, IL: Southern Illinois University Press, 1980.

DeConick, April. *The Thirteenth Apostle: What the Gospel of Judas Really Says.* Rev. edn, London and New York: Continuum, 2009.

Dzon, Mary. 'Cecily Neville and the Apocryphal *Infantia Salvatoris* in the Middle Ages.' *Mediaeval Studies* 71 (2009): 235–300.

Ehrman, Bart D. *Lost Christianities: The Battles for Scripture and the Faiths We Never Knew.* Oxford and New York: Oxford University Press, 2003.

———, ed. *Lost Scriptures: Books That Did Not Make It into the New Testament.* Oxford and New York: Oxford University Press, 2003.

Ehrman, Bart D. and Zlatko Pleše, eds. *The Apocryphal Gospels: Texts and Translations.* Oxford and New York: Oxford University Press, 2011.

Elliott, J. Keith. 'The Non-Canonical Gospels and the New Testament Apocrypha: Currents in Early Christian Thought and Beyond.' Pages 1–12 in *The Non-Canonical Gospels.* Edited by Paul Foster. London and New York: T&T Clark, 2008.

———, ed. *A Synopsis of the Apocryphal Nativity and Infancy Narratives.* New Testament Tools and Studies 34. Leiden/Boston: Brill, 2006.

————, ed. *The Apocryphal New Testament: A Collection of Apocryphal Christian Literature in an English Translation Based on M. R. James.* Oxford: Clarendon, 1993. Corrected paperback edn, 2005.

————. *The Apocryphal Jesus: Legends of the Early Church.* Oxford and New York: Oxford University Press, 1996.

Erbetta, Mario. *Gli apocrifi del Nuovo Testamento.* 4 vols. Turin: Marietti, 1966–81.

Evans, Craig A. *Fabricating Jesus: How Modern Scholars Distort the Gospels.* Downers Grove, IL: InterVarsity Press, 2006.

Fabricius, Johann Albert, ed. *Codex apocryphus Novi Testamenti.* 2 vols. Hamburg: Schiller, 1703.

Foster, Paul. *The Apocryphal Gospels: A Very Short Introduction.* Oxford and New York: Oxford University Press, 2009.

Halkin, François. 'Une Vie grecque de sainte Marie-Madeleine.' *Analecta Bollandiana* 105 (1987): 5–23.

Hedrick, Charles W. and Paul A. Mirecki. *Gospel of the Savior: A New Ancient Gospel.* California Classical Library. Santa Rosa, CA: Polebridge, 1999.

Hennecke, Edgar, ed. *Neutestamentliche Apokryphen in deutscher Übersetzung.* Tübingen: Mohr (Siebeck), 1904. 2nd edn, 1924.

————. *Handbuch zu Neutestamentlichen apokryphen in deutscher Übersetzung.* Tübingen: Mohr (Siebeck), 1904.

Hennecke, Edgar and Wilhelm Schneemelcher, eds. *New Testament Apocrypha.* 2 vols. Trans. R. McL. Wilson. London: Luttersworth Press, 1963/5. Translation of *Neutestamentliche Apokryphen in deutscher Übersetzung.* 2 vols. 3rd edn, Tübingen: Mohr (Siebeck), 1959/64.

Hill, George F. 'The Thirty Pieces of Silver.' *Archaeologia* 59 (1905): 235–54.

Himmelfarb, Martha. *Tours of Hell: An Apocalyptic Form in Jewish and Christian Literature.* Philadelphia: University of Pennsylvania Press, 1983.

Hock, Ronald F. *The Infancy Gospels of James and Thomas.* The Scholars Bible 2. Santa Rosa, CA: Polebridge, 1996.

Holmes, Michael W., ed. and trans. *The Apostolic Fathers.* Grand Rapids, MI: Baker Books, 1999.

Izydorczyk, Zbigniew. 'The Unfamiliar *Evangelium Nicodemi.*' *Manuscripta* 33 (1989): 169–91.

James, M. R. *Apocrypha Anecdota.* Texts and Studies 2.3. Cambridge: Cambridge University Press, 1893.

Jeremias, Joachim, ed. *Unknown Sayings of Jesus.* 2nd English edn, London: SPCK, 1964.

Bibliography

Jones, F. Stanley. *An Ancient Jewish Christian Source on the History of Christianity: Pseudo-Clementine Recognitions 1.27–71.* Christian Apocrypha Series 2; Texts and Translations 37. Atlanta, GA: Scholars Press, 1995.

King, Karen L. *What Is Gnosticism?* Cambridge, MA: Harvard University Press, 2003.

Klauck, Hans-Josef. *The Apocryphal Acts of the Apostles: An Introduction.* Trans. Brian McNeil. Waco, TX: Baylor University Press, 2008. Translation of *Apokryphe Apostelakten. Eine Einführung.* Stuttgart: Katholisches Bibelwerk, 2005.

——. *Apocryphal Gospels: An Introduction.* Trans. Brian McNeil. London and New York: T&T Clark, 2003. Translation of *Apokryphe Evangelien. Eine Einführung.* Stuttgart: Katholisches Bibelwerk, 2002.

Klijn, A. F. J. *Jewish-Christian Gospel Tradition.* Vigiliae christianae, Supplements 17. Leiden: Brill, 1992.

Koester, Helmut. *Ancient Christian Gospels: Their History and Development.* London: SCM Press, 1990.

——. 'Apocryphal and Canonical Gospels.' *Harvard Theological Review* 73 (1980): 105–30.

Köstenberger, Andreas J. and Michael J. Kruger. *The Heresy of Orthodoxy: How Contemporary Culture's Fascination with Diversity Has Reshaped our Understanding of Early Christianity.* Wheaton, IL: Crossway, 2010.

Kraus, T. J., M. J. Kruger and T. Nicklas, eds. *Gospel Fragments.* Oxford Early Christian Gospel Texts. Oxford and New York: Oxford University Press, 2008.

Krosney, Herbert. *The Lost Gospel of Judas: The Quest for the Gospel of Judas Iscariot.* Washington, DC: National Geographic, 2006.

Landau, Brent. *Revelation of the Magi: The Lost Tale of the Wise Men's Journey to Bethlehem.* San Francisco: HarperCollins, 2010.

McCulloch, John A. *The Harrowing of Hell: A Comparative Study of an Early Christian Doctrine.* Edinburgh: T&T Clark, 1930.

MacDonald, Dennis R. *The Legend and the Apostle: The Battle for Paul in Story and Canon.* Philadelphia: Westminster John Knox, 1983.

McDonald, Lee Martin. *Formation of the Bible: The Story of the Church's Canon.* Peabody, MA: Hendrickson, 2012.

——. *The Origin of the Bible: A Guide for the Perplexed.* London and New York: T&T Clark, 2011.

Markschies, Christoph and Jens Schröter, eds. *Antike christliche Apokryphen in deutscher Übersetzung.* Vol. 1. Tübingen: Mohr (Siebeck), 2012.

Metzger, Bruce M. *The Bible in Translation: Ancient and English Versions.* Grand Rapids, MI: Baker, 2001.

Meyer, Marvin, ed. *The Nag Hammadi Scriptures: The International Edition*. New York: HarperCollins, 2007.

Michel, Charles and Paul Peeters, eds. *Évangiles apocryphes*. 2 vols. Textes et documents pour l'étude historique du Christianisme 13 and 14. Paris: Librairie Alphonse Picard & Fils, 1911/14.

Migne, Jacques-Paul, ed. *Dictionnaire des Apocryphes*. 2 vols. 1856. Repr. Turnhout: Brepols, 1989.

Miller, Robert J., ed. *The Complete Gospels: The Scholars Version*. 1992. 4th edn, Salem, OR: Polebridge, 2010.

Mingana, Alphonse. 'Apocalypse of Peter.' Pages 93–449 in *Woodbrooke Studies: Christian Documents in Syriac, Arabic, and Garshuni*. Vol. 3. Edited by Alphonse Mingana. Cambridge: Cambridge University Press, 1931.

––––. 'A New Life of John the Baptist.' Pages 138–45, 234–87 in *Woodbrooke Studies: Christian Documents in Syriac, Arabic, and Garshuni*. Vol. 1. Edited by Alphonse Mingana. Cambridge: Cambridge University Press, 1927.

Moraldi, Luigi, ed. *Apocrifi del Nuovo Testamento*. 2 vols. Classici delle religioni 24. Turin: Unione Tipografico – Editrice Torinese, 1971; 2nd edn in 3 vols, Casale Monferrato: Piemme, 1994.

Orlandi, Tito. 'The Library of the Monastery of St. Shenute at Atripe.' Pages 211–31 in *Perspectives on Panopolis: An Egyptian Town from Alexander the Great to the Arab Conquest*. Edited by A. Egberts, B. P. Muhs and J. van der Vliet. Papyrologica Lugduno-Batava 31. Leiden: Brill, 2002.

Pagels, Elaine. *The Gnostic Gospels*. New York: Vintage Books, 1979.

Parsons, Peter. *City of the Sharp-nosed Fish: Greek Lives in Roman Egypt*. London: Weidenfeld & Nicolson, 2007.

Pearson, Birger A. *Ancient Gnosticism: Traditions and Literature*. Minneapolis: Fortress Press, 2007.

Phillips, George. *The Doctrine of Addai the Apostle Now First Edited in a Complete Form in the Original Syriac with an English Translation and Notes*. London: 1876. Repr. as George Howard, ed. *The Teaching of Addai*. Texts and Translations 16, Early Christian Literature Series 4. Chico, CA: Scholars Press, 1981.

Piovanelli, Pierluigi. 'Exploring the Ethiopic *Book of the Cock*, An Apocryphal Passion Gospel from Late Antiquity.' *Harvard Theological Review* 96 (2003): 427–54.

Price, Robert M. *Secret Scrolls: Revelations from the Lost Gospel Novels*. Eugene, OR: Wipf & Stock, 2011.

Robinson, James. *The Story of the Bodmer Papyri*. Eugene, OR: Cascade, 2011.

Schmidt, Carl and Violet MacDermot. *Pistis Sophia*. Nag Hammadi Studies 9. Leiden: Brill, 1978.

Schneemelcher, Wilhelm, ed. *New Testament Apocrypha*. 2 vols. Trans. R. McL. Wilson. Rev. edn, Louisville, KY: Westminster John Knox, 1991/2. Translation of *Neutestamentliche Apokryphen in deutscher Übersetzung*. 2 vols. 5th edn, Tübingen: Mohr (Siebeck), 1987/9.

Shoemaker, Stephen J. *Ancient Traditions of the Virgin Mary's Dormition and Assumption*. Oxford Early Christian Studies. Oxford: Oxford University Press, 2002.

Skarsaune, Oskar and Reidar Hvalvik, eds. *Jewish Believers in Jesus*. Peabody, MA: Hendrickson, 2007.

Soskice, Janet. *The Sisters of Sinai: How Two Lady Adventurers Discovered the Hidden Gospels*. New York: Alfred A. Knopf, 2009.

Speake, Graham. *Mount Athos: Renewal in Paradise*. New Haven: Yale University Press, 2002.

Terian, Abraham, ed. *The Armenian Gospel of the Infancy*. Oxford and New York: Oxford University Press, 2008.

Tischendorf, Constantin von, ed. *Evangelia apocrypha*. Leipzig: Mendelssohn, 1853; 2nd edn, 1876.

——. *Apocalypses apocryphae*. Leipzig: Mendelssohn, 1866.

——. *Acta apostolorum apocrypha*. Leipzig: Mendelssohn, 1851.

Tuckett, Christopher, ed. *The Gospel of Mary*. Oxford Early Christian Gospel Texts. Oxford and New York: Oxford University Press, 2007.

Voragine, Jacobus de. *The Golden Legend: Readings on the Saints*. 2 vols. Translated by William Granger Ryan. Princeton: Princeton University Press, 1993.

Williams, Michael A. *Rethinking 'Gnosticism': An Argument for Dismantling a Dubious Category*. Princeton, NJ: Princeton University Press, 1996.

Witherington, Ben. *The Gospel Code: Novel Claims about Jesus, Mary Magdalene and Da Vinci*. Downers Grove, IL: InterVarsity Press, 2004.

Index of apocryphal texts

Index of apocryphal texts